PROFIT PL

Books in the series

Improving Food and Beverage Performance (Waller)
Managing Facilities (Jones and Jowett)
Managing People (Riley)
Marketing (Fewell and Wills)
Profit Planning (Harris)
Successful Pubs and Inns (Sargent and Lyle)

PROFIT PLANNING

Second edition

Peter Harris

Series Editor: John O'Connor

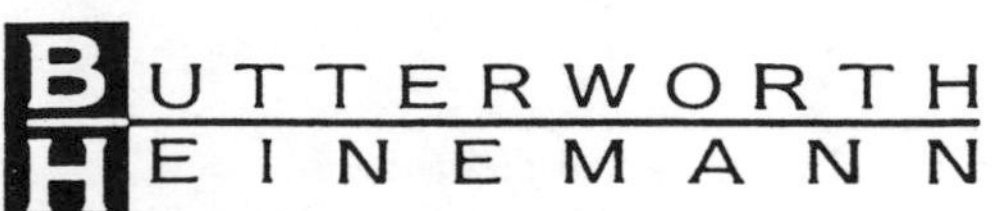

OXFORD AMSTERDAM BOSTON LONDON NEW YORK PARIS
SAN DIEGO SAN FRANCISCO SINGAPORE SYDNEY TOKYO

To Elaine and Samantha Kate

Butterworth-Heinemann
An imprint of Elsevier Science
Linacre House, Jordan Hill, Oxford OX2 8DP
200 Wheeler Road, Burlington MA 01803

First published 1992
Reprinted 1994, 1996, 1998
Second edition 1999
Reprinted 2001, 2003

British Library Cataloguing in Publication Data
Harris, Peter J. (Peter James), *1944–*
Profit planning – 2nd ed.
1. Hotel management
I. Title. II. Caterer and Hotelkeeper magazine
647′.0681

ISBN 0 7506 4528 8

Typeset by Avocet Typeset, Brill, Aylesbury, Bucks
Printed and bound in Great Britain by
Biddles Ltd, *www.biddles.co.uk*

Contents

Preface to the second edition

This book is primarily written for practising managers and entrepreneurs operating in a wide variety of hotel and restaurant establishments. Many of the publications available to hospitality managers tend to focus on the theoretical areas of accounting and financial management, whereas this book emphasizes the more practical aspects of day-to-day profit planning in hotel and catering undertakings.

The terms 'hotel' and 'restaurant', used in the text, can be interpreted in a broad context. Many hospitality businesses incorporate the provision of rooms, food and beverage services and, therefore, the examples and illustrations can readily be translated into licensed house management, industrial and institutional catering, clubs and so on. It is hoped that the reader will find the explanations and examples to be practical and straightforward in approach with a minimum of theory and technical jargon.

Revisions for this edition include the partial rewriting of Chapter 1 Key features of hotel and restaurant operations; the revision of the cash flow statements section in Chapter 2 Review of hospitality financial statements; the extension of RevPAR calculations and the inclusion of an interpretation of results section in Chapter 3 Understanding results; the addition of hotel CVP applications in Chapter 5 Planning for profit; and the updating of Chapter 8 Budgets and forecasting and Chapter 9 Getting the information we need.

No publication can claim to be solely due to the efforts and experience of a single author, and so I would like to acknowledge the support and assistance given to me by a number of people. First, my colleague Cathy Burgess, at Oxford Brookes University, who contributed Chapter 8 Budgets and forecasting, and Tracy Jones, at Cheltenham and Gloucester College of Higher Education, who contributed Chapter 11 Getting the information we need. I would like to acknowledge the work of Professor Richard Kotas, formerly of the University of Surrey, who developed the idea of profit sensitivity analysis. I would also like to thank John O'Connor, Emeritus Professor at Oxford Brookes University, and Jacquie Shanahan at Butterworth-Heinemann, who initially persuaded me to write this book and supported me throughout. Additionally, my thanks go to Catherine Clarke and Tim Goodfellow of Butterworth-Heinemann for their guidance in preparing this revised edition. Finally, I am indebted to my wife Elaine for wordprocessing and proof-reading the original manuscript.

My single wish is that readers continue to find this book to be a practical aid to profit planning.

Peter Harris
July, 1999

1 Key features of hotel and restaurant operations

Before we consider profit planning it is worthwhile to pause, 'step back' and review our perspective of the hotel and catering industry. This is particularly relevant in financial terms for if profit planning is to be applied effectively in hotels and restaurants then attention should be given to the type of product we offer, the kinds of activity undertaken and the method of operation used. Once these features have been established the appropriate profit planning techniques can be selected and adapted to suit the particular business situation under consideration.

A new look at hotel and restaurant activities

The main activities found in the hotel and catering industry relate to the provision and service of rooms, food and beverages. As hotels typically incorporate all three areas we will use hotels as an example.

Traditionally, operating a hotel has been compared to running a domestic household, each providing sleeping accommodation, food and refreshment, and managing a hotel has been seen as only an extension of home management. At first glance this appears to be true, but on closer examination we will see that it is not an accurate assessment. Furthermore, such a view exposes a lack of understanding of both the nature of hotel and home management and the different demands placed on hotel and household managers.

Hotel and restaurant undertakings are commercial enterprises that trade in the business environment and, like any other concerns, are subject to the complexities of economic and market forces. We compete with one another, and with other kinds of business, for consumer spending. In order to maintain our market position – or even survive – we constantly need to plan, monitor and improve our products and services. We also need to keep abreast of technological and managerial developments that will increase efficiency and maintain a competitive edge. Thus, while at first sight hotels may in principle be similar to the domestic domicile, in practice they are firmly locked into the commercial and industrial world. To some extent the misconceived analogy of homes and hotels sheds light on some of the problems of innovation, quality and efficiency with which the hotel industry has, to some extent, been associated.

Within the provision of the mainstream rooms, food and beverage services a hotel can be seen to encapsulate three different kinds of business activity under one roof, namely those of service, production and retail. As these activities have significant implications on managing profitability, let us consider them in the context of a hotel.

Room letting activity

As reflected in Figure 1.1 the provision of rooms constitutes a 'near pure' intangible service industry product. The letting of a bedroom represents the sale (or rental) of space over a period of time. The guest checks into the hotel, spends the night and leaves the next morning. There is no tangible product purchased by the guest, simply a memory of the experience. This service product is comparable to an airline flight where a seat is rented, to car rental or to a visit to a lawyer or accountant.

Beverage service activity

The provision of alcoholic beverages represents a service industry product that contains a retail function. This activity includes our buying, displaying, merchandising and selling various drink products in a way similar to departmental stores or shops. Unlike room letting the beverage product is somewhat more tangible, but the service element is present in that drinks are poured and served (delivered) to customers. In addition, beverage provision contains an important stock management component, depicted in Figure 1.1. We need to maintain an effective beverage stock management system in order to satisfy customer demands while at the same time minimizing the level of capital investment.

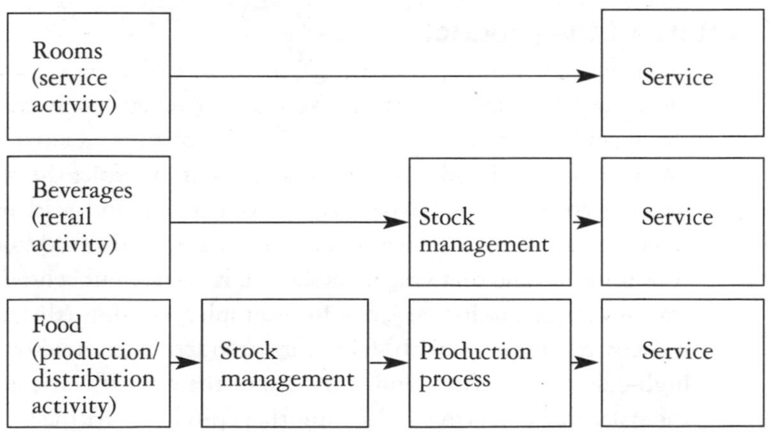

Figure 1.1 A hotel operation showing key activities and the associated elements

Food service activity

As indicated in Figure 1.1, the provision of food represents a service industry product that includes a production function.

The production function comprises the purchase and conversion of raw materials (ingredients) into finished products such as dishes and meals which, although normally consumed almost simultaneously, are distributed and/or sold through a process that has parallels with car manufacture or domestic appliance production. The product is fairly tangible and has a significant service component in that dishes are served (delivered) to customers. In addition, the provision of food contains an important stock management component, similar to that for beverages, and usually requires considerable food preparation and production facilities in order for the product to be produced.

Thus, the above view of room, food and beverage activities serves to highlight the deceptive complexity of operating a hotel. The wide range of commercial and industrial activities represent a considerable challenge to managers in their bid to offer a 'seamless' and competitive 'total hotel product' experience to the consumer.

Nature of the product

Over the years other industries have sought to overcome some of the operational, marketing and financial problems still faced by many of our hotel and catering concerns. For example, the traditional cobbler's shop where shoes were made and sold has largely gone out of existence. Production has been divorced from consumption, and footwear manufacture is carried out centrally by a few large producers. This, for example, has allowed shoemakers to dispense with footwear production in relatively high-cost city locations and concentrate their efforts on using the space for promoting and selling their products. At the same time footwear manufacturers have been able to produce and distribute their products from a more cost-effective location, and also to benefit from the economies of scale. This has also occurred in the drinks industry, where large brewers have evolved the production and distribution of beer to public houses and other licensed premises. However, it is more difficult to apply the principle to hotels and restaurants because the nature of the meal product usually demands that at least some production facilities are located on site where food is consumed.

The approach to profit planning and control

A sound insight into the organization and methods of operation used in hotel and restaurant concerns is important if we are to determine the appropriate approach to accounting and profit planning. A fundamental principle to bear in mind is that the accounting and financial management methods used should be designed to suit the method of operation found in a particular business. If this principle is not consciously observed the accounting contribution is likely to prove ineffective and counter-productive in planning and controlling profits. However, the fact that hotel and catering undertakings contain features observed in other industries should not deter us from making comparisons and applying selected approaches in our own establishments and organizations.

A review of hotel and restaurant characteristics

Having considered the key features of hotel and restaurant operations at the establishment (unit) level it is useful if we briefly reflect upon the key characteristics of the industry in general. These also have a direct bearing on profit planning and are outlined below.

Fixed capacity

Hotels contain a 'stock of bedrooms' which in the short-run are fixed (static). Therefore, in periods of high demand room reservation requests often have to be refused with the subsequent loss of revenue. A similar, though not so severe 'fixed capacity' situation is also to be found with regard to restaurant and bar seating. However, by comparison, a manufacturer has greater flexibility to increase the number of production shifts or acquire improved machinery in order to expand capacity and increase output, whereas a hotel is rarely able to increase the number of times a room is sold per day beyond a single letting.

In periods of low demand a hotel can reduce some labour costs, but the large majority of other expenses such as administration, energy, maintenance, rent, interest and depreciation are still present. Thus, the need for accurate forecasting and effective marketing to generate revenue is paramount in maintaining and improving profits.

Perishability

Hotels experience 'absolute perishability' in terms of room stocks. An unsold room represents an irretrievable loss of revenue. By comparison shops, for example, have the potential to offer special promotions and 'sales' to sell unsold stock items at a later date. Raw and prepared food items are also perishable, though clearly to a lesser extent than rooms. Here there is the dual need for us to develop effective stock planning and control procedures in addition to sound marketing.

Erratic demand

Hotels and restaurants often experience significant fluctuations in demand. For example, breakfast and dinner periods may be busy, while lunch periods may be relatively quiet. During the week some hotels achieve high occupancies from business clientele, but may be virtually empty at weekends. Over a year other hotels may attain high occupancies at peak holiday times while suffering low take-up in the off-season. This three-dimensional type of demand necessitates an innovatory approach to product/service development, marketing and profit planning in an effort to increase business levels during low periods.

Product range

While manufacturing firms are associated with high volume and relatively limited product choice, hotels and restaurants are characterized by their low volume and wide choice. In many cases restaurants offer three and four different product lists, in the form of menus, per day, i.e. breakfast, lunch, afternoon tea and dinner. With a relatively wide range of choice within each menu even the larger establishments experience a comparatively low volume per menu item. In recent years the emergence of fast food, speciality and coffee-shop restaurants have ameliorated the situation, but the basic characteristic still widely persists. Optimizing relative product profitability in these circumstances is a challenging exercise.

Real-time activity

Another characteristic encountered in hotel and catering operations is the immediacy of the activities. Unlike the situation where the customer wishes to acquire a car or washing machine and is prepared to take delivery at a later date, the customer arriving for a room, meal or drink requires the product immediately and cannot be expected to wait until a later date. Thus, the 'real time' pressure element of hotel and restaurant activities results in a fairly stressful working environment where sound planning and organization is required in order to reduce pressure and facilitate smooth operating conditions. The ability to manage this aspect of operations has considerable implications on medium and long-term profitability.

Labour intensity

The 'service nature' of hotel and restaurant services often dictates that activities are carried out manually, rather than by machines. In recent years considerable efforts and resources have been devoted to the simplification of production and service methods. Examples include the introduction of convenience foods, self-service and short-order systems, and fast food restaurants with their manufacturing-type processes, but due to the economics of size and consumer expectation little progress has been made. Also, the rendering of services is an area in which machines have, so far, been unable to replace human beings to any appreciable extent. Hence, the control of labour costs by effective human resource management is particularly important for profit optimization in such a labour intensive industry.

Location

The hotel and restaurant business is a market-centred activity and as such establishments generally need to be located where the products and services are consumed. Frequently they are situated on prime sites that attract high purchase and operating costs. A hotel or restaurant built in a low-cost industrial estate or deprived area is unlikely to prove to be economically viable because the consumer will normally demand pleasant surroundings close to local amenities.

Size

As a result of the diffuse nature of the hotel and catering industry individual establishments are comparatively small when compared with other industries. Even the largest units are relatively small when compared with many engineering or manufacturing plants. It is, therefore, often difficult for hotels and restaurants to benefit from the economies of scale and to generate sufficient revenues required to employ highly trained, highly paid management and staff. Size has been overcome to some extent by, for example, the chains developing buying power through centralized purchasing and some independent undertakings forming marketing consortiums to promote their services more effectively, but it remains a problematic area in terms of optimizing profitability.

Production and consumption

As mentioned earlier, in hotels and restaurants production and consumption are often synonymous. Food is prepared on site and usually consumed immediately or soon afterwards. Some large catering operations such as hospitals, universities and employee feeding facilities have central cook-freeze and cook-chill units where they produce for stock and distribute to the various outlets. However, hotel restaurants and stand-alone restaurants usually produce and sell for consumption in the same arena. As a consequence of this we find that hotels and restaurants contain some of the most expensive 'factories' – in the form of production kitchens – in the world, such as those in Park Lane and Mayfair in the West End of London. This can be partly overcome by separating production from consumption and locating production centrally in a lower cost area. This not only enables additional 'high cost' space to be given over to revenue generation activities, but also provides an opportunity to benefit from the economies of scale. For instance, centrally produced chicken and duck portions allow the otherwise wasted giblets to be used to produce pâté, an up-market food item with a high profit mark-up; a profitable activity that adds value to the process rather than cost. However, unlike the cobbler who was able to totally dispose of his workshop, restaurants still usually, at the very least, require satellite finishing kitchens at the point of sale.

Capital intensity

Another feature of hotel and catering establishments relates to the amount of capital investment. Large sums are frequently required to be committed, particularly in hotel projects, of which the greater proportion is tied up in land, buildings, furniture and fittings. Prominent locations alone add to the magnitude of the financial sums involved and subsequently contribute to the high level of operating costs. In addition, compared with some industries the ratio of sales to capital employed is relatively low, resulting in the problem of insufficient cash flow for debt (loan) servicing, particularly during the early years of operation.

Cost structure

Finally, as we move more specifically towards profit planning methods and techniques contained in subsequent chapters of this book, we can observe a particularly significant characteristic present in the industry, namely that of 'cost structure'. The cost structure of an undertaking is determined by the 'nature of the product/service' which in turn is reflected in the distribution of fixed and variable costs to total cost. A business with a large proportion of fixed cost to total cost is said to have a high fixed-cost structure. Conversely, a business that contains a high proportion of variable costs is regarded as having a low fixed-cost structure. The cost structure of a business is best illustrated by cost-volume-profit (CVP) graphs (traditionally known as break-even graphs).

Examination of the CVP graphs in Figure 1.2 reveals the following:

- Business A has a higher proportion of fixed costs than Business B.
- Business A must achieve a higher level of sales to break even and generate a profit.
- If both businesses experience a similar change in demand the impact on profit will be greater for Business A.

Thus, in view of its higher break-even point and greater sensitivity to changes in demand, Business A is more dependent on revenue generation than Business B. Furthermore, because of its lower proportion of variable costs, Business A has only limited scope to improve profits by cost control procedures and techniques. We can therefore conclude that due to its dependence on market demand, Business A should adopt a market oriented approach to profit planning. This does not imply that cost control is not important – all costs are required to be controlled – but that, in the case of Business A, a greater emphasis should be placed on the revenue side of the business.

In general we can conclude that the higher the proportion of fixed costs, the greater the dependence on market demand and, therefore, the greater the need for market orientation. By contrast, the higher the proportion of variable costs the less the dependence on market demand and the greater the need for cost orientation. Thus, as Business B has a lower break-even point, less sensitivity to fluctuations in demand and more scope

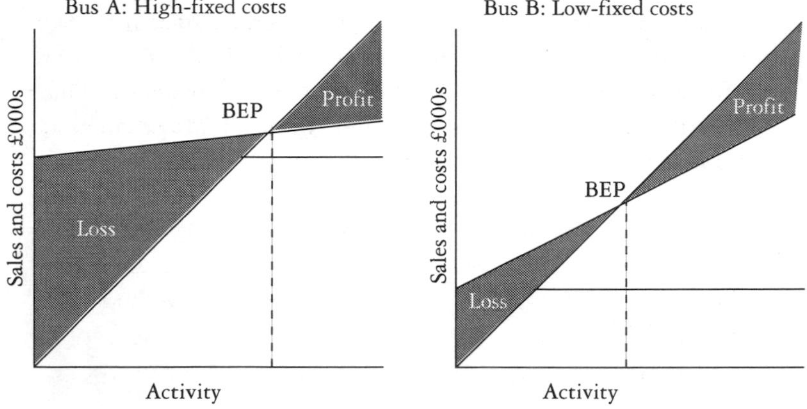

Figure 1.2 Cost structure of the two businesses

for cost control it should adopt a cost oriented approach to profit planning.

High-volume catering facilities with low average spends tend to be cost oriented. Examples are employee feeding, hospitals, schools, colleges and universities. Hotels and restaurants with their relatively low volume and high average spends are more market oriented. Indeed, the higher the average spend, the greater the degree of market orientation as the proportion of fixed costs increases and the variable costs pale into relative insignificance.

Compared with manufacturing industry, service industries such as the hotel industry tend to experience relatively high fixed-cost structures. The reason for this is that a large proportion of hotel costs are contained in the infrastructure of the building and the provision of the fundamental service facilities offered therein (and not directly affected by the volume of individual products and services themselves) and, therefore, are not affected by changes in the volume of business achieved. These costs include 'building occupancy costs' such as rent and rates, loan interest, building and contents insurance, and depreciation and 'operating costs' such as administration, marketing, repairs and maintenance, and energy. Thus, unless there is a dramatic change in the level of business generated these fixed costs will remain relatively static year on year. By comparison, a larger proportion of the total costs of producing a manufactured product is incorporated in the product itself, in the form of direct materials, direct labour and direct expenses. This, together with the relatively high volumes of production, results in a lower fixed-cost structure.

2 Review of hospitality financial statements

The key financial statements produced from an accounting system which are relevant to hotel and restaurant managers are the

- profit and loss statement;
- balance sheet;
- cash flow statement.

These statements are fundamental to profit planning and control of business operations and form the basis to help us measure, analyse and interpret our operating results in financial terms.

Profit and loss statements

The profit and loss statement is our primary financial report. It summarizes the revenues generated and expenses incurred during a period and indicates the profit or loss that results.

Basic profit and loss statements

The structure of the traditional profit and loss statement has derived from the presentation required by manufacturing

	£
Sales	300,000
Less: cost of sales	90,000
Gross profit	210,000
Less: operating expenses	150,000
Net profit	£ 60,000

Figure 2.1 Basic profit and loss statement

firms. In its basic form the profit and loss statement appears in Figure 2.1.

We must take into account a number of accounting principles and conventions when preparing the statement, the most important of which is the 'matching', also known as the 'accural' principle. This requires that only revenues generated during a period and expenses incurred in the generation of those revenues should be included (matched) in the profit and loss statement, irrespective of when cash is received or paid. For instance, referring to Figure 2.1 we may find that part of the revenue of £300,000 generated during the period was received after the period had ended. The amount outstanding will affect the cash position at the end of the period, but will not affect the reported profit of £60,000. The matching principle is crucial in determining the true profit or loss for a given period.

We can consider another example where the matching principle plays an important role in determining gross profit, shown in Figure 2.2. Notice that the cost of sales figure of £90,000 has been analysed to reveal that £100,000 worth of stock purchases was made during the period. However, in the light of the stocks on hand at the beginning and end of the period we can determine that only £90,000 worth of stock was consumed (cost of sales) in generating the sales of £300,000. Thus we can see that gross profit results from sales revenue less the cost of generating those sales and *not*, as is sometimes thought, sales revenue less the cost of purchases.

Service industry type of profit and loss statements

We find that the presentation of traditional profit and loss statements reflect manufacturing industry methods which place emphasis on individual product costs and gross profits. However, the activities carried out in service industry firms, such as hotel and catering, are usually operated on a departmental rather than product basis and, therefore, it is more appropriate to classify revenue and expenses according to departments.

Expenses that are directly related to specific revenue-producing departments are known as 'direct expenses' whereas expenses not so related, but that benefit the firm as a whole, are termed 'indirect expenses' or 'overheads'. The basic structure of a service industry profit and loss statement is shown in Figure 2.3. Note that while other industries rely on gross profit as a basic measure of profitability, service industry firms emphasize departmental profit that contributes to an overall net profit. Relating direct expenses to departments provides us with an effective basis on which to evaluate departmental performance.

	£	£
Sales		300,000
Less: cost of sales:		
Opening stock	10,000	
Purchases	100,000	
	110,000	
Less: closing stock	20,000	90,000
Gross profit		210,000
Less: operating expenses		150,000
Net profit		£ 60,000

Figure 2.2 Profit and loss statement

	£
Departmental revenues	300,000
Less: departmental expenses	140,000
Departmental profit	160,000
Less: indirect expenses	100,000
Net profit	£ 60,000

Figure 2.3 Service industry profit and loss statement

Hotel profit and loss statements

All the previously mentioned operating activities and industry characteristics referred to in Chapter 1 are taken into account in the Uniform System of Accounts for the Lodging Industry (USALI), an all-inclusive format that includes most of the sources of revenue and expenses encountered in hospitality undertakings. The USALI profit and loss statement layout designed for our internal management use is shown in Figure 2.4.

Referring to Figure 2.4, this presentation of revenue and expense items makes it possible for us effectively to measure all the major activities in our own hotel operation. Notice that indirect expenses are divided into two groups known as 'undistributed operating expenses' and 'fixed charges'.

		£
Section 1	Operating departments	
	Departmental revenue	300,000
	Less: direct expenses	140,000
	Departmental profit	160,000
Section 2	Less: undistributed operating expenses (controllable)	30,000
	Profit before fixed charges	130,000
Section 3	Less: fixed charges (non-controllable)	70,000
	Net profit	£ 60,000

Figure 2.4 Uniform System of Accounts for Hotels (USALI) profit and loss statement (internal management layout)

Departmental profit

Section 1 of the profit and loss statement contains all the revenue-producing departments of the hotel. Direct expenses are allocated to the respective departments and the departmental profit is determined by subtracting direct expenses from departmental revenues. The departmental profit provides us with the basis on which to evaluate departmental performance.

Profit before fixed charges

In Section 2 we find the undistributed operating expenses are deducted from departmental profit to give 'profit before fixed charges', more commonly referred to in practice as Gross Operating Profit (GOP). This provides us with a key measure of the operating efficiency for the entire hotel. The undistributed operating expenses are incurred for the benefit of the hotel as a whole, and are not usually apportioned to operated departments.

Net profit

Finally, in Section 3 the fixed charges are deducted from the profit before fixed charges in order to determine our net profit. The fixed charges are not operating expenses as they basically represent the occupation costs of the hotel building and are normally outside the control of operating managers, such as the general manager and department heads, at the property level. As a result, fixed charges should not be taken into account in the overall evaluation of operating performance of managers at the unit level, but must of course be taken into account in the overall evaluation of financial performance.

In terms of managerial operating emphasis the USALI statement is designed to encourage us to optimize departmental profit. This is not the same as maximizing revenues or minimizing direct expenses. Rather, it is the attainment of an optimum combination of revenues and expenses, which together provide us with the greatest total departmental profit contribution towards the recovery of undistributed operating expenses and fixed charges, in order to achieve an adequate residual net profit for the owners (shareholders).

Responsibility format

The format of the statement is designed in terms of managerial responsibility. This means that departmental managers are responsible for their respective department profits, the hotel general manager is responsible for the profits before fixed charges, and top management, i.e. the directors or owners, are responsible for net profit. A USALI profit and loss statement for our internal management use is illustrated in Figure 2.5. It is worth noting that this statement is designed to include all the possible revenues and expenses found in hotels and can readily be adapted to our own particular hotel requirements.

Note that the direct departmental expenses are analysed into cost of sales, payroll and related expenses, and other expenses. The major undistributed operating expenses mainly consist of administration, marketing, energy and property maintenance. Fixed charges include property rates and insurance, loan interest and depreciation of assets, e.g. buildings, equipment and furniture.

Restaurant profit and loss statements

A restaurant profit and loss statement is similar in principle to the hotel statement. The layout recommended in the Uniform System of Accounts for Restaurants (USAR) for our internal management use is outlined in Figure 2.6.

As with the hotel profit and loss statement the format of the restaurant statement is also designed in terms of managerial responsibility. Thus, the restaurant manager is usually responsible for profit before fixed charges, i.e. food and beverage revenues, cost of sales and gross profit, plus the controllable

Operating departments	Net revenues	Cost of sales	Payroll and related expenses	Other expenses	Profit (loss)
	£	£	£	£	£
Rooms	150,000	-	37,000	12,000	101,000
Food and beverages	100,000	40,000	23,000	10,000	27,000
Other, e.g. telephone	50,000	-	15,000	3,000	32,000
Total	300,000	40,000	75,000	25,000	160,000
Undistributed operating expenses:					
Administration				7,500	
Marketing				9,000	
Energy				10,000	
Property maintenance				3,500	30,000
Profit before fixed charges					130,000
Rates and insurance				26,000	
Loan interest				30,000	
Depreciation				14,000	70,000
Net profit for period					60,000

Figure 2.5 Hotel profit and loss statement (internal management layout)

	£
Revenue:	
Food	12,000
Beverages	8,000
Total revenue	20,000
Cost of sales:	
Food	5,000
Beverages	4,000
	9,000
Gross profit	11,000
Controllable expenses:	
Payroll and related expenses	3,500
Direct operating expenses	1,250
Music and entertainment	400
Marketing	600
Energy	350
Administration	420
Repairs and maintenance	380
	6,900
Profit before fixed charges	4,100
Rent, business rate and insurance	1,300
Loan interest	700
Depreciation of assets	100
	2,100
Net profit for period	2,000

Figure 2.6 Restaurant profit and loss statement (internal management use)

expenses. The directors or owners are, however, responsible for net profit, i.e. all revenues and expenses, plus the fixed charges. Again, the statement can easily be adapted to suit the requirements of our own particular restaurant operation.

Balance sheets

Whereas the profit and loss report summarizes the revenues generated and expenses incurred (accrued) throughout a period, the balance sheet shows a snapshot of the financial position of a business at the end of a period. Unlike profit and loss statements, balance sheet layout and presentation is not generally influenced by the kind of industry. We find that the items in a balance sheet are grouped into assets, liabilities and capital, as shown in Figure 2.7.

Balance Sheet		
Long-term items	Owners' capital + profits long-term liabilities e.g. loans	Fixed assets e.g. premises equipment furniture
Short-term items	Current liabilities e.g creditors overdraft	Current assets e.g food stocks debtors cash

Figure 2.7 Balance sheet

Long-term items

Fixed assets are items owned by a business for use in the provision of products and services and are expected to benefit the business over several years. The purchase of these items is 'capital expenditure' compared to the purchase of items for immediate consumption in the provision of meals and services which is 'revenue expenditure'. Fixed assets include items such as freehold and leasehold premises, equipment and furniture, and china, glass, cutlery and linen. Long-term liabilities normally take the form of bank and other loans which are repayable in future years. Capital is a more permanent item which, along with profits, represents the owner's investment in the business.

Short-term items

Current assets and current liabilities are of a less permanent nature. They include food and beverage stocks, debtors, cash and bank balances, creditors and bank overdrafts, all of which are needed to service our routine hotel and restaurant activities of providing rooms, meals and drinks. The difference in value between the value of current assets and current liabilities is called 'working capital'.

Balance sheet layout

There are various ways of arranging the groups of assets and liabilities in a balance sheet, but as we shall see they basically fall into two layouts, namely the traditional or so-called 'horizontal' layout, or the more contemporary or 'vertical' layout. Figures 2.8 and 2.9 illustrate the two kinds of layout. Comparison of the two presentations shows that we read the horizontal balance sheet across the sheet, whereas with the vertical style layout we read down the sheet much as we would read a page in a book. Both approaches are equally acceptable as there is no overall argument in favour of choosing one in preference to the other. The important point to bear in mind when we read a balance sheet is that the figures only represent the values of the assets, liabilities and capital of a business at a single point in time, which is normally the last day of the financial period. Therefore, if we read a balance sheet a few weeks or months after the stated date we should be aware that the values will have changed.

Cash flow statements

We have seen earlier that the profit and loss statement summarizes the revenue generated and expenses incurred during a period in order to show us the profit or loss that has accrued. By comparison, the cash flow statement provides a summary of how cash has been generated and used during a period.

	£	£		£	£	£
					Total	
Owner's capital		300,000	Fixed assets:	Cost	Depreciation	Net
Profit for period		60,000	Freehold property	400,000	50,000	350,000
Owners' interest (equity)		360,000	Equip. & furniture	250,000	100,000	150,000
			China, glass etc	80,000	30,000	50,000
				730,000	180,000	550,000
Long-term liabilities:						
Bank loan		200,000				
		560,000				
Current liabilities:			Current assets:			
Creditors	13,000		Food & bev. stocks		20,000	
Bank overdraft	27,000	40,000	Debtors		28,000	
			Cash balances		2,000	50,000
Total liabilities		£600,000	Total assets			£600,000

Figure 2.8 Balance sheet (horizontal layout)

Fixed assets:	£ Cost	£ Total Depreciation	£ Net
Freehold property	400,000	50,000	350,000
Furniture & equipment	250,000	100,000	150,000
China, glass etc.	80,000	30,000	50,000
	730,000	180,000	550,000
Current assets:			
Food & beverage stocks	20,000		
Debtors	28,000		
Cash balances	2,000	50,000	
Less current liabilities:			
Creditors	13,000		
Bank overdraft	27,000	40,000	
Working capital			10,000
			560,000
Financed by:			£
Owners' capital			300,000
Profit for period			60,000
Owners' interest (equity)			360,000
Long-term liabilities:			
Bank loan			200,000
			560,000

Figure 2.9 Balance sheet (vertical layout)

It also explains the change, in cash and bank balances, that has occurred between the current and previous balance sheets.

An additional value of the cash flow statement is that it helps us to understand why the cash position at the end of a period is different (assuming it is) from the profits achieved during the period.

By referring to the cash flow statement presented in Figure 2.10 we can see why the cash position has deteriorated by £35,000 during the period and turned an £8,000 cash surplus at the outset into a £27,000 overdraft at the end of the period:

- The £99,000 net cash inflow generated from operations result from adjusting the profit (before interest and tax – though there is no tax payable in this example) of £90,000, by adding back the period depreciation charge £14,000 (a non-cash item) and the decrease in food and beverage stocks of £10,000, and deducting the increase in debtors £8,000 and decrease in creditors £7,000.
- From the £99,000 net cash flow we deduct loan interest paid of £30,000 (loan interest and tax are shown separately as they are not regarded as a expenses incurred in operating a business, but as financial expenses) and the purchase of furniture of £119,000, and adding the additional funds obtained from an increase in the bank loan of £15,000 leaving a net cash flow outwards for the period of £35,000. Thus, the £35,000 net cash outflow will represent the decrease in the cash position between the balance sheets at the beginning and end of the period.

In Figure 2.10 we can see that the major reason for the deterioration in cash was due to heavy capital expenditure on furniture. Without this item the cash balance would grow substantially. However, in any event it is unlikely that the profit earned during the period would have equalled the cash at the end of the period. Thus the cash flow statement not only highlights the causes of the change in the cash position, but in addition provides an insight into the relationship between profit and cash.

Please note: if you wish to obtain copies of the Uniform Systems of Accounts for Hotels and Restaurants the addresses are as follows:

1 Hotel Association of New York City Inc., *Uniform System of Accounts for the Lodging Industry*, 9th ed., 1996. Published by the Educational Institute of the American Hotel and Motel Association, 1407 South Harrison Road, P.O. 1240, East Lansing, Michigan 48826, USA.

2 National Restaurant Association, *Uniform System of Accounts for Restaurants*, 5th ed., 1983 (311 First Street, NW, Washington, DC 20001, USA).

	£	£	£
Balance at bank (end of previous period)			8,000
Net cash flow from operations:			
Profit for period	90,000		
+ Depreciation	14,000		
+ Decrease in f & b stocks	10,000		
– Increase in debtors	(8,000)		
– Decrease in creditors	(7,000)		
Net cash inflow (outflow)		99,000	
Tax paid:		0	
Return on invest/servicing loans:			
– Loan interest paid		(30,000)	
Investing activities:			
– Purchase of furniture		(119,000)	
Financing activities:			
+ Increase in bank loan		15,000	
Net cash inflow (outflow) during period			(35,000)
Balances at bank (end of current period) overdraft			(27,000)

Figure 2.10 Cash flow statement

3 Understanding results

Most operating results are presented in the form of profit and loss statements and balance sheets, both of which comprise a collection of totals taken from the bookkeeping and accounting system. However, if we examine report totals alone their meaning and significance are not readily apparent. In order to determine the consequence of results we need to identify reported amounts which have a direct and understandable relationship between them.

Using ratios

Basically, a ratio expresses a mathematical relationship between one value and another. For instance, if we wish to learn more about total food cost incurred over a period we should relate food cost of sales to food revenue because, among other things, food cost depends on the volume of sales.

As we shall see, ratios are relatively simple to calculate, but their interpretation demands a sound understanding of the particular business under review. Ratios point managers towards clues and symptoms of underlying operating conditions that would otherwise go undetected by observing their individual components alone. Thus, a working knowledge of ratios is important if we are to understand our results.

Kinds of ratio

We can group ratios into distinct categories according to the type of information required. A common grouping is as follows:

- liquidity ratios;
- asset management ratios;
- debt management ratios;
- profitability ratios;
- operating ratios.

In order to assist us in understanding how to calculate and interpret the ratios we will use an example of the assumed Garden House Hotel, the results of which are given in Figures 3.1 and 3.2.

Liquidity ratios

Liquidity ratios provide us with an indication of the short-term solvency of a business, in other words the ability of a business to meet its immediate obligations.

Current ratio

The current ratio gives an overview of a firm's liquidity by showing the relationship between current assets and current liabilities as follows:

$$\text{Current ratio} = \frac{\text{Current assets at end of period}}{\text{Current liabilities at end of period}}$$

$$= \frac{£234{,}000}{£234{,}000}$$

$$= 1{:}1$$

	Year 1	Year 2
Fixed assets (net)	£	£
Freehold land and buildings	598,000	780,000
Equipment and furniture	140,000	200,000
China, glass, cutlery	25,000	20,000
	763,000	1,000,000
Current assets		
Food stocks	5,000	13,000
Beverage stocks	10,000	63,000
Debtors	24,000	129,000
Short-term deposits/ investments	5,000	25,000
Cash at bank	101,000	4,000
	145,000	234,000
Total assets	908,000	1,234,000
Owners' equity		
Capital	436,000	551,000
Retained profit	82,000	209,000
	518,000	760,000
Long-term liabilities		
15% loan (secured on freehold property – year 10)	240,000	240,000
Current liabilities		
Creditors and accruals	142,000	211,000
Bank overdraft	8,000	23,000
	150,000	234,000
Total liabilities and owners' equity	£908,000	£1,234,000

Figure 3.1 Garden House Hotel
Balance sheet as at 31 December

We can see that the Garden House Hotel's current ratio at the end of Year 2 indicates that it has £1 worth of current assets to cover each pound of current liabilities. So it appears that the hotel can fund its short-term debts out of short-term assets, but is it able to pay its creditors?

Rooms department:	£
Sales revenue	700,000
Payroll and related expenses	119,000
Other expenses	63,000
Total expenses	182,000
Department profit	518,000
Food and beverage department:	
Food revenue	400,000
Beverage revenue	300,000
Total revenue	700,000
Food cost	180,000
Beverage cost	100,000
Total cost	280,000
Gross profit	420,000
Payroll and related expenses	210,000
Other expenses	35,000
Total expenses	245,000
Department profit	175,000
Total department profits	693,000
Undistributed operating expenses:	
Admin and general	102,000
Marketing	23,000
Energy	28,000
Property operation and maintenance	20,000
Total UOE	173,000
Profit before fixed charges	520,000
Occupation expenses	230,000
Loan interest	36,000
Total fixed charges	266,000
Net profit before tax	254,000
Tax (50%)	127,000
Net profit after tax	£127,000

Figure 3.2 Garden House Hotel
Profit and loss statement for year ended 31 December – Year 2

Acid test ratio

A better indicator of a firm's ability to repay its short-term debts is the acid test ratio, sometimes called the quick assets ratio. This ratio shows the relationship between the quick assets, i.e. debtors, short-term deposits/investments and cash (or current assets minus stocks), and current liabilities as follows:

$$\text{Acid test ratio} = \frac{\text{Quick assets at end of period}}{\text{Current liabilities at end of period}}$$

$$= \frac{\pounds 158{,}000}{\pounds 234{,}000}$$

$$= 0.68 : 1$$

We can see that our hotel's acid test ratio at the end of Year 2 shows it has £0.68 for each pound of current liabilities. Theoretically there should be £1 of quick assets to cover each pound of current liabilities, but in practice, providing it has arranged a bank overdraft, our hotel would be able to operate with an acid test ratio of less than 1 : 1. Many businesses rely on overdrafts to fund short-term operations. The problem is that an overdraft can be called in at short notice and this could cause a business to become insolvent because it is unable to pay its immediate bills.

Asset management ratios

This group of ratios give an indication of how effectively we utilize the assets at our disposal.

Stock turnover ratio

The basic stock turnover ratio is calculated in the following manner:

$$\text{Stock turnover ratio} = \frac{\text{Cost of sales}}{\text{Average stock}}$$

The average stock is determined by adding start of the year to end of the year figures and dividing by two, as follows:

$$\text{Average stock} = \frac{\text{Opening stock + Closing stock}}{2}$$

In the hotel and restaurant business the two key stocks that should be closely controlled are food and beverage:

$$\text{Food stock turnover ratio} = \frac{\pounds 180{,}000}{\frac{(\pounds 5{,}000 + \pounds 13{,}000)}{2}} = \frac{\pounds 180{,}000}{\pounds 9{,}000} = 20 \text{ times}$$

So, the Garden House Hotel turned over its food stock twenty times during Year 2. As this ratio is not very user-friendly, we can express it in terms of the number of days' supply of food stock as follows:

Food stocks ratio:

$$\text{Number of days' supply} = \frac{\text{Days per year}}{\text{Stock turnover}} = \frac{365}{20} = 18.25 \text{ days}$$

This tells us that we are holding approximately two and a half weeks of food stocks. Depending on the class of restaurant we would normally expect to hold between one and two weeks' stocks, so it might be advantageous for the hotel to investigate the possibility of reducing food stocks to a lower level. This in turn would improve the acid test ratio by making additional cash available for paying creditors or reducing the overdraft.

$$\text{Beverage stock turnover ratio} = \frac{\pounds 100{,}000}{\frac{(\pounds 10{,}000 + \pounds 63{,}000)}{2}} = \frac{\pounds 100{,}000}{\pounds 36{,}500} = 2.74 \text{ times}$$

Or expressed in terms of the number of days' supply:

Beverage stocks ratio:

$$\text{Number of days' supply} = \frac{\text{Days per year}}{\text{Stock turnover}} = \frac{365}{2.74} = 133 \text{ days}$$

The beverage stock ratios show the hotel is carrying on average nineteen weeks' or approximately four and a half months' stocks of beverage. Again, depending on the kind of establishment, we would normally expect the figure to be between one and three months. Therefore, at over four months' supply the beverage stock is out of control due mainly to the high year-end figure of £63,000, and should be reduced immediately. This should significantly improve the hotel's acid test ratio.

It is difficult to generalize about stock ratios, but an important point to bear in mind is that normally the more up-market the establishment the lower the stock turnover ratio or the higher the number of days' supply ratio. This is because the higher average spend restaurants and licensed premises tend to hold a wider variety of stocks, some of which contain a considerable amount of high-cost items, e.g. wines and liqueurs, and this, coupled with the fact that numbers of covers are often relatively low, will cause beverage stock ratios in particular to turn over relatively slowly.

Debtor ratios

These ratios are similar in principle to the stock ratios and show how effectively we manage our credit control. The debtor turnover ratio for Year 2 is calculated in the following manner (assuming credit sales is 30 per cent of sales):

$$\text{Debtor turnover ratio} = \frac{\text{Credit sales}}{\text{Average debtors}} = \frac{£1{,}400{,}000 \times 30\%}{\frac{(£24{,}000 + £129{,}000)}{2}} = \frac{£420{,}000}{£76{,}500} = 5.49 \text{ times}$$

The average debtors is obtained by adding start of the year to end of the year figures and dividing by two. If we express the debtors turnover ratio in terms of the average collection period for debts the result will be as follows:

Debtors ratio:

$$\text{Average collection period} = \frac{\text{Days per year}}{\text{Debtors turnover}} = \frac{365}{5.49} = 67 \text{ days}$$

This figure indicates the hotel is on average taking over nine weeks (more than two months) to collect its debts. The problem has been caused by the dramatic increase in debtors in Year 2 and signals an urgent need to review the hotel's credit control procedures. This figure should be reduced to four to six weeks.

Fixed asset turnover ratio

This ratio indicates how effectively we are utilizing fixed assets to generate sales revenue:

$$\text{Fixed asset turnover ratio} = \frac{\text{Sales revenue}}{\text{Average fixed assets}} = \frac{\pounds 1,400,000}{\dfrac{(\pounds 763,000 + \pounds 1,000,000)}{2}} = \frac{\pounds 1,400,000}{\pounds 881,500} = 1.6 \text{ times}$$

The ratio tells us that our hotel is achieving £1.60 sales for each one pound invested in fixed assets. In the hotel industry this figure can range from around one to over two times a year, so our hotel seems to be managing its fixed assets fairly effectively.

Total asset turnover ratio

This ratio indicates how effectively we utilize total fixed and current assets in generating sales revenue:

$$\text{Total asset turnover ratio} = \frac{\text{Sales revenue}}{\text{Average total assets}}$$
$$= \frac{£1{,}400{,}000}{\frac{(£908{,}000 + £1{,}234{,}000)}{2}}$$
$$= \frac{£1{,}400{,}000}{£1{,}071{,}000}$$
$$= 1.3 \text{ times}$$

Note the average total assets are determined by adding start of year to end of year figures and dividing by two.

The total assets turnover ratio informs us that the hotel is achieving £1.30 sales for each one pound invested in total assets. In the hotel industry this figure tends to vary from half to around two times a year, so our hotel appears to be managing its total assets quite effectively.

Debt management ratios

We have seen how liquidity ratios provide an indication of the short-term solvency of a business. Debt management ratios give us an idea of the long-term solvency of a business.

Solvency ratio

This ratio measures the long-term solvency of a business as follows:

$$\text{Solvency ratio} = \frac{\text{Total assets at end of period}}{\text{Total liabilities at end of period}}$$
$$= \frac{£1{,}234{,}000}{£474{,}000}$$
$$= 2.6 : 1$$

This means that if our hotel were not profitable and were forced to close down, there would be £2.60 of assets (at book value) for every one pound of liabilities. Thus, long-term creditors can be reasonably assured of receiving something in the event of liquidation and sale of the Garden House Hotel assets. We can see that all debts would be covered even if we sold the hotel's assets for under half of their book value.

Gearing ratio

The gearing, or leverage, ratio is used to show the relationship between the amount of fixed interest and fixed dividend capital and owners' interest (equity) as follows:

$$\text{Gearing ratio (a)} = \frac{\text{Fixed interest capital}}{\text{Owners' interest (equity)}}$$
$$= \frac{£240{,}000}{£760{,}000}$$
$$= 0.32 : 1 \text{ or } 32 \text{ per cent}$$

Our hotel has a gearing ratio that indicates that for each £1 of owners' equity it has obtained 32p of borrowed capital. It may be easier to understand if we express the ratio another way, as shown below:

$$\text{Gearing ratio (b)} = \frac{\text{Fixed interest capital}}{\text{Total long-term capital}}$$
$$= \frac{£240{,}000}{£760{,}000 + £240{,}000)}$$
$$= \frac{£240{,}000}{£1{,}000{,}000}$$
$$= 0.24 : 1 \text{ or } 24 \text{ per cent}$$

Thus we can see the hotel has borrowed 24 per cent of its long-term capital. There is no hard and fast rule for this ratio but it is generally accepted that a business with a gearing ratio (b) of 40 per cent or less would be regarded as a low-geared company whereas a business with a ratio of above 40 per cent would be regarded as highly geared.

Interest coverage ratio

This ratio gives an indication of a firm's ability to meet its interest payments out of current profits, and as such is a rough indicator of long-term solvency.

$$\text{Interest coverage ratio} = \frac{\text{Net profit before interest and tax}}{\text{Annual interest expense}} = \frac{£290{,}000}{£36{,}000} = 8 \text{ times}$$

Thus, after all other expenses have been met the Garden House Hotel has sufficient profits to cover the annual interest charge eight times.

Profitability ratios

A business may show a 'profit' in its profit and loss statement and yet not be regarded as 'profitable'. The reason for this lies at the very heart of ratios. In order to determine the meaning and significance of a profit figure it needs to be expressed in relation to some other figure such as sales revenue, total assets or owners' equity.

Net profit ratio

This is a key ratio which provides us with an indication of the overall operating efficiency of senior management and is in effect the net return on sales:

$$\text{Net profit ratio} = \frac{\text{Net profit before tax}}{\text{Total sales revenue}} = \frac{£254{,}000}{£1{,}400{,}000} = 18.1 \text{ per cent}$$

This shows us that our model is generating £0.18 net profit for every £1 sales revenue. Fixed charges are not controllable by the general manager of a hotel but they must be included in the measurement of overall profitability. This ratio tends to vary from 5–20 per cent in hotels and restaurants.

Profit before fixed charges ratio

This ratio, also known as the operating efficiency ratio, is another important profitability ratio because it gives an indication of the overall business operating efficiency of the unit manager:

$$\text{Profit before fixed charges ratio} = \frac{\text{Profit before fixed charges}}{\text{Total sales revenue}} = \frac{£520{,}000}{£1{,}400{,}000} = 37 \text{ per cent}$$

Fixed charges are omitted as they are not normally controllable by unit managers. The ratio tells us that £0.37 profit before fixed charges is achieved from each £1 of sales revenue. In hotels this figure is around 30-40 per cent, so that the Garden House Hotel is operating satisfactorily at the unit level. *Note:* Profit before fixed charges is also referred to as 'gross operating profit' or 'GOP'.

Return on total assets ratio

This ratio gives us an indication of how effectively we manage total assets in generating profit. It is also a useful guide in assessing the advisability of obtaining more debt financing. The ratio is calculated as follows:

$$\text{Return on total assets ratio} = \frac{\text{Profit before interest and tax}}{\text{Average total assets}} = \frac{£290{,}000}{\frac{(£908{,}000 + £1{,}234{,}000)}{2}}$$

$$= \frac{£290,000}{£1,071,000}$$

$$= 27 \text{ per cent}$$

Average total assets are determined by adding the start of year and end of year figures and dividing by two.

Our hotel's assets are being used to generate an annual return of £0.27 before interest on each £1 of assets. Interest is omitted so we can determine the true profit earning ability of the assets, without being influenced by the amount of debt financing (loans). This is a useful rough indicator when deciding on the purchase and funding of new assets. The resulting ratio of 27 per cent provides a basis on which the earning ability of business assets can be compared with the interest rate for debt capital used in financing the assets. For example, if we planned an extension to the Garden House Hotel and the current interest rate for debt financing was 14 per cent we could reasonably assume the new building would generate a return sufficient to cover the interest rate and leave a profit for the owners.

Net return on total assets ratio

This ratio also gives an indication of how we manage total assets in generating profit. It is also useful in assessing the likelihood of obtaining more equity financing. The ratio is calculated as shown below:

$$\text{Net return on total assets ratio} = \frac{\text{Net profit after tax}}{\text{Average total assets}}$$

$$= \frac{£127,000}{\frac{(£908,000 + £1,234,000)}{2}}$$

$$= \frac{£127,000}{£1,071,000}$$

$$= 11.9 \text{ per cent}$$

This shows us that our hotel is achieving £0.119 after tax profits per annum for every £1 invested in total assets. If we wished to finance a new extension, would equity funding be a viable option? Owners receive dividends from after tax profits, so assuming the new asset achieves a similar return the owners could anticipate a satisfactory return.

Return on owners' equity ratio

This ratio shows how effectively we generate profits from operations in terms of the owner's total investment and is determined as follows:

$$\text{Return on equity ratio} = \frac{\text{Net profit after tax}}{\text{Average owner's equity}}$$

$$= \frac{\pounds 127{,}000}{\dfrac{(\pounds 518{,}000 + \pounds 760{,}000)}{2}}$$

$$= \frac{\pounds 127{,}000}{\pounds 639{,}000}$$

$$= 19.9 \text{ per cent}$$

The result shows that the Garden House Hotel is generating an annual return of almost £0.20 for each £1 of owners' equity. What figure should the ratio be? If the full benefit is to be attained, the owners should compare the rate of return with other alternative investment opportunities.

Operating ratios

Hotel and restaurant operations are concerned with the provision and service of rooms, food and beverages. In financial terms this results in generating revenue and incurring expenses. Operating ratios are used to monitor the relationships in these two areas.

Sales mix ratio

This ratio shows us the composition of total sales revenue and is calculated by expressing department sales as a percentage of total sales. The Garden House Hotel sales mix is as follows:

Department:	£	%
Rooms	700,000	50.0
Food	400,000	28.6
Beverage	300,000	21.4
Total	1,400,000	100.0

We can also express sales mix ratios as follows:

$$\text{Food revenue to F \& B revenue} = \frac{\text{Food revenue}}{\text{F \& B revenue}} = \frac{£400,000}{£700,000} = 57 \text{ per cent}$$

$$\text{Beverage revenue to F \& B revenue} = \frac{\text{Beverage revenue}}{\text{F \& B revenue}} = \frac{£300,000}{£700,000} = 43 \text{ per cent}$$

$$\text{F \& B revenue to total revenue} = \frac{\text{F \& B revenue}}{\text{Total revenue}} = \frac{£700,000}{£1,400,000} = 50 \text{ per cent}$$

In order to determine whether the hotel is optimizing its sales mix we should compare the results against some yardstick such as budgeted sales mix or industry averages. Clearly we should try to improve profit by increasing sales in the departments (or products and services) with the higher contribution margin/gross profit.

Other operating ratios can be considered on a department basis. In order to explain these ratios we will use the additional assumed data from the Garden House Hotel given in Figure 3.3.

Rack rate per room: Single			£45
Double			£55
Number rooms available in hotel:	Single	20	
	Double	40	60
Number rooms sold in Year 2			16,425
Number guests staying in Year 2			21,850
Number food covers sold in Year 2			40,000
Number of restaurant seats			100

Figure 3.3 Garden House Hotel
Additional data

Rooms department

$$\text{Average achieved room rate (AARR)} = \frac{\text{Rooms revenue}}{\text{Rooms sold}} = \frac{£700{,}000}{16{,}425} = £42.62$$

The trend of the average achieved room rate is important. It can be influenced by directing selling efforts into higher priced rooms and by increasing the rate of double occupancy (see below). The figure is normally calculated on a daily basis and averaged for weekly, monthly and annual periods. It is a particularly useful ratio where a hotel operates differential rates for different rooms and offers discounted rates.

$$\text{Room occupancy percentage} = \frac{\text{Rooms sold}}{\text{Rooms available}} = \frac{16{,}425}{(60 \times 365)} = 75 \text{ per cent}$$

Rooms temporarily unavailable due to redecoration or refurbishment are normally included in the rooms available figure. However, rooms used permanently for staff should be omitted. The figure is an important basic indicator of rooms capacity utilization. Room occupancy percentages are normally calculated on a daily basis and averaged for weekly, monthly and annual periods.

$$\text{Double occupancy percentage} = \frac{\text{Number of rooms double occupied}}{\text{Number of rooms sold}}$$

$$= \frac{21{,}850 - 16{,}425}{16{,}425}$$

$$= \frac{5{,}425}{16{,}425}$$

$$= 33 \text{ per cent}$$

The ratio tells us that 33 per cent of all rooms sold were occupied by two people. It indicates the extent to which the hotel is maximizing the use of available bed capacity and, where differential rates are charged for double occupancy, is reflected in the average achieved room rate.

Yield percentage

As an overall indication of the level of business achieved, actual revenue is related to total potential revenue calculated on the basis of 100 per cent room occupancy, 100 per cent double occupancy or whatever total guest occupancy is for the hotel, and will normally use rack rate (tariff) net of distributable service charge, value added tax and breakfast (if included) to give maximum attainable revenue.

$$\text{Yield percentage} = \frac{\text{Rooms revenue}}{\text{Maximum potential rooms revenue}}$$

Maximum potential rooms revenue is calculated as follows:

		£
20 single rooms × £45 × 365	=	328,500
40 double rooms × £55 × 365	=	803,000
Maximum potential rooms revenue		1,131,500
Hence, the yield percentage	=	£700,000 / 1,131,500
	=	61.9 per cent

The yield percentage is a more global and sensitive ratio than other room statistics. Notice that although the Garden House Hotel has achieved 75 per cent in terms of room occupancy, in potential revenue terms it represents the considerably lower figure of 61.9 per cent.

Revenue per available room

$$\text{Revenue per available room (RevPAR)} = \frac{\text{Rooms revenue}}{\text{Number of rooms available}} = \frac{£700{,}000}{60} = £11{,}667 \text{ (annually)}$$

RevPAR is a combination of the average achieved room rate (AARR) and the room occupancy percentage. This ratio overcomes the limitations of using the AARR and occupancy percentage individually where, for instance, high occupancy may be achieved at the expense of a low AARR or, conversely, a high AARR at the expense of a low occupancy. RevPAR is determined either by dividing rooms revenue by the number of rooms available (as above) or by multiplying room occupancy by the AARR (Room occupancy 0.75 x AARR £42.62 = RevPAR per day £31.965). Thus, RevPAR per annum is £31.965 x 365 days = £11,667. The trend of this ratio is particularly useful for comparison with similar establishments in an organization or with industry averages.

$$\text{Cost per available room (CostPAR)} = \frac{\text{Rooms expenses}}{\text{Number of rooms available}} = \frac{182{,}000}{60} = £3033.33 \text{ (annually)}$$

Again, as with the revenue per available room, this ratio is useful for comparison with similar establishments in a company or with industry averages.

$$\text{Labour cost percentage} = \frac{\text{Rooms payroll and related expenses}}{\text{Rooms revenue}} = \frac{£119{,}000}{£700{,}000} = 17 \text{ per cent}$$

Labour represents a significant cost in the hospitality industry. The trend of this ratio is important and should be closely controlled weekly or monthly against budget.

Food and beverage department

$$\text{Average food spend (restaurant)} = \frac{\text{Food revenue}}{\text{Number of covers}} = \frac{£400{,}000}{40{,}000} = £10 \text{ per cover}$$

$$\text{Average beverage spend (restaurant)} = \frac{\text{Beverage revenue}}{\text{Number of covers}} = \frac{£300{,}000}{40{,}000} = £7.50 \text{ per cover}$$

This ratio should preferably be calculated by meal period, by day and by outlet, and the trend monitored closely.

$$\text{Seat turnover} = \frac{\text{Number of covers}}{\text{Seats available}} = \frac{40{,}000}{100 \times 365} = 1.1 \text{ times}$$

This ratio should also be calculated by meal period, by day and by outlet and the trend monitored closely in conjunction with the average spend figures. A declining seat turnover may indicate that high prices or poor quality are deterring customers.

$$\text{Food cost percentage} = \frac{\text{Cost of food sold}}{\text{Food revenue}} = \frac{£180{,}000}{£400{,}000} = 45 \text{ per cent}$$

$$\text{Beverage cost percentage} = \frac{\text{Cost of beverage sold}}{\text{Beverage revenue}}$$

$$= \frac{£100,000}{£300,000}$$

$$= 33.3 \text{ per cent}$$

Food and beverage costs rank among the highest costs of operating a restaurant and therefore warrant close control. Assuming there are no dramatic changes in sales mix or selling prices food and beverage cost percentages provide a fairly effective method of monitoring purchasing, pilferage and wastage of materials. The percentages are normally calculated on a weekly or monthly basis.

$$\text{Labour cost percentage} = \frac{\text{F \& B payroll and related expenses}}{\text{F \& B revenue}}$$

$$= \frac{£210,000}{£700,000}$$

$$= 30 \text{ per cent}$$

Again, an important ratio that should be controlled weekly or monthly against budget.

Other operating ratios

$$\text{Number of rooms serviced per employee} = \frac{\text{Number of rooms serviced}}{\text{Number of employees}}$$

$$\text{Number of covers served per employee} = \frac{\text{Number of covers served}}{\text{Number of employees}}$$

$$\text{Revenue per employee} = \frac{\text{Food and beverage revenue}}{\text{Number of employees}}$$

These ratios are essentially determined to assess productivity and should be compared by outlet against an established standard on a daily, weekly or monthly basis.

Interpretation of results

As we have seen, ratios can help us to understand what our results mean in technical and business terms. The asset management, profitability and operating ratios tend to focus on trading efficiency, i.e. the more operational side of the business relating to revenue and expenses, represented by the profit and loss statement. In contrast, the liquidity and debt management ratios tend to focus on short-term and long-term solvency respectively, i.e. the more financial management side of an undertaking relating to assets and liabilities, represented by the balance sheet.

In the case of the Garden House Hotel results we can see that operating profitability (GOP 37% and net profit 18.1%) and debt management (long-term solvency 2.6:1, gearing 24% and interest cover at eight times) appears sound, as does long-term and overall asset utilization (fixed asset turnover 1.6:1 and total asset turnover 1.3:1). However, working capital management, in relation to short-term assets such as stocks, debtors and cash, is less effective (food and beverage stocks at 18.25 days and 133 days respectively, debtor collection 67 days and acid test £0.68:1). Thus, management should review food and beverage purchasing policy, with a view to reducing stocks, and review credit control procedures in order to release cash and, therefore, improve the liquidity position indicated by the acid test ratio. If this is effected successfully the overall financial position of the hotel will be seen to be very satisfactory.

Yield management

While a detailed examination of yield management is beyond the scope of this book its importance warrants a brief introduction to the approach.

In essence yield management is a technique that assists in the maximization of revenues from the sale of a product or service that contains the following characteristics:

- perishability over the passage of time;
- fixed capacity.

Clearly, hotel rooms fit this profile. An unsold room is a sale lost for ever. Also we are unable to add additional rooms simply because a major sporting or business event happens to be taking place in the vicinity. So what is yield management and how can it assist managers to maximize room revenue? Yield management is concerned with control over rates and restrictions to occupancy in order to achieve the maximum possible gross revenue from all sources per period of time.

Fundamentally, yield management works as follows:

- when demand exceeds supply, the objective focuses on decisions to maximize room rate;
- when supply exceeds demand, the objective changes to the maximization of room occupancy, even to some extent, at the expense of average rate.

Traditionally, we have measured success in terms of average rate and occupancy, but is this effective? Let us consider a simple example. Assume we have a 200 room hotel with the last three days' results as follows:

	Occupancy %	*Average rate*
Tuesday	53.8	£111.50
Wednesday	71.0	£84.35
Thursday	92.0	£65.20

Which result is most appealing? At first glance Wednesday seems to have a more balanced result than the other two days. Tuesday has a high average room rate, but a low occupancy percentage. Thursday has a high occupancy, but a low average rate. However, if we calculate the total room revenue per day we find they each yields approximately £12,000. We may argue that Tuesday is more profitable because it has the lowest variable costs, or that Thursday is more favourable because it has the best potential to generate food and beverage sales. Both points of view are plausible, but for most hotels the profitability of the three days will essentially be the same.

To measure the underlying equality of the three days' results we need to determine the yield percentage (illustrated previously in this chapter). If we assume all rooms were sold at the top rates, giving £24,000 revenue per day, the yield percentages will be as follows:

$$\text{Yield percentage} = \frac{\text{Rooms revenue}}{\text{Maximum potential rooms revenue}}$$

$$= \frac{\pounds 12{,}000}{\pounds 24{,}000}$$

$$= 50 \text{ per cent}$$

We may debate the relative merits of each of the day's earnings, but few would contest that, say, 55 or 60 per cent yield was less acceptable than 50 per cent. Thus, yield management is concerned with maximizing the combined effects of rate and occupancy, and not their separate results.

4 Monitoring progress

Sources of comparison

The value of financial and other operating information is fairly limited if there is no means of comparison to assess its significance. In order to obtain the benefits of operating information we should take the opportunity to compare current results against some form of yardstick. The main sources of information available for comparison are as follows:

- past results;
- budgeted performance;
- intra-company results;
- industry studies.

We will briefly consider how each of these potential yardsticks can help in monitoring the progress of a business.

Past results

We can compare current operating performance with past results, as this will give us an indication of the changes that have taken place in an operation, for example growth or contraction. Such a comparison is useful for planning purposes.

However, care should be exercised when evaluating changes as previous results may have been abnormally good or poor.

Budgeted performance

Another measure of operating performance is the comparison of current results against budget. This assumes the presence of realistic budgets that are periodically updated. Regular comparison of actual with budgeted results will provide us with an effective basis for controlling revenue and costs.

Intra-company results

If a hotel or restaurant is part of a chain we can compare the performance with those of similar operations. However, although the other operations may be similar in terms of product, service and price they may, for instance, be much larger or smaller in size to the operation under consideration. In this case a proper basis for comparison should be established (explained later) so that results produced are meaningful.

Industry studies

A growing number of industry surveys are becoming available for various sectors of the hospitality industry. These studies often include current operating statistics and economic trends. In many cases there is some attempt to make the statistics more useful for comparison purposes by dividing the total sample into different categories such as hotels by geographical location, number of rooms, and average room rate.

Due to confidentiality operating results cannot be disclosed for particular establishments and so industry statistics are usually published in the form of averages.

Averages used in industry studies

The most commonly used averages in hospitality industry reports and studies are the 'arithmetic mean' and the 'median'. They are representative values of a survey sample, or to be more precise they are measures of 'central tendency'. By central tendency we mean the tendency of observations in a sample to centre around a particular value rather than spread themselves evenly across the range.

Arithmetic mean

The mean is what is normally called 'the average' in elementary arithmetic. It is calculated by adding together all the observed values and dividing by the number of observations. Hence, we would calculate the mean restaurant sales value per day over a one week period as follows:

Mon.	Tues.	Wed.	Thurs.	Fri.	Sat.	Sun.
£430	£380	£520	£350	£420	£790	£470

$$\frac{430 + 380 + 520 + 350 + 420 + 790 + 470}{7} = 480$$

Thus, the arithmetic mean is £480 per day.

We observe that no day had sales of £480, but the observed values tend to centre around £480.

Median

The median (from the Latin for 'middle') is found by arranging the observed values in ascending or descending order, known as a 'distribution', and locating the middle item. In fact the median is whatever value splits a distribution in half. There should be as many observed values greater than the median as there are less than the median. Thus, if we arrange our daily restaurant sales in a distribution we can determine the median as follows:

350 380 420 430 470 520 790

Thus, the median sales value is £430 per day.

Where the number of observed values is even there would be no observed value with an equal number of values each side of it. In such cases, the median is quoted as the value which is half-way between the middle items. So if the Saturday restaurant sales of £790 had not been part of the sample our distribution would look like this:

350 380 420 430 470 520

and the median sales value would be calculated as follows:

$$\frac{420 + 430}{2} = £425 \text{ per day}$$

Which average?

As a measure of central tendency the mean has several advantages, the main one being that it is fairly stable from one sample to another, that is, if we take a number of samples from the same population (say all the restaurants in a chain) their means are likely to differ less than the medians. Thus, a sample mean would give us the most reliable estimate of central tendency in the restaurant chain.

There are, however, some situations where it may be appropriate to concentrate on the sizes of the middle values (medians). For example, take the case of our restaurant sales. The mean daily sales is £480 and the median is £430, so which average would give a better idea of typical restaurant sales? Would it be the mean or the median? In this case the median would give a better idea of typical daily restaurant sales. The mean has been affected considerably by the extreme value of £790 so it is less typical of daily sales. Thus, the median is usually preferable where there are a few extreme (high or low) values observed.

Comparing operating results

If we wish to compare current (actual) results with either past results or budget we would calculate the difference as follows:

Actual result – Budget result = Absolute difference (or variance)

For example, if actual sales revenue was £49,000 and budgeted sales revenue was £50,000 the variance would be:

Actual		Budget		Absolute variance
£49,000	–	£50,000	=	–£1,000

The variance is denoted by a minus sign because there was a sales shortfall of £1,000. If, on the other hand, we want to know a little more about the shortfall in sales we can calculate the relative variance in addition to the absolute variance as follows:

Actual		Budget		Absolute variance		Relative variance
£49,000	–	£50,000	=	– £1,000	=	2 per cent

The relative variance, which is expressed as a percentage, is calculated by the following formula:

$$\frac{\text{Actual} - \text{Budget}}{\text{Budget (base)}} \times \frac{100}{1}$$

$$= \frac{(£49{,}000 - £50{,}000)}{£50{,}000} \times \frac{100}{1} = 2 \text{ per cent}$$

It is important to note that you should always express the relative difference (variance) as a percentage of the item that you regard as the yardstick (or base), in this case budgeted sales. The relative variance of 2 per cent gives us an additional insight into the result. Although the sales shortfall of £1,000 may be judged as a fairly considerable amount in absolute terms, as a percentage it represents only a 2 per cent drop in business. It is, therefore, important to keep the comparison of results in a proper perspective in order to avoid misinterpretation of the magnitude of differences.

Common-size statements

If we wish to compare current results between two restaurants in the same company or with industry averages then the comparison can be limited by significant differences in size. Where this is so there is little value in comparing absolute amounts. However, the relative value of absolute amounts is readily comparable. We can achieve this by expressing each value in the profit and loss statement as a percentage of total sales and each value in the balance sheet as a percentage of total assets. When we express financial statements in percentage terms they are referred to as 'common-size statements'.

Comparing in-company results

Let us take the example of the assumed Eatin Restaurant Company that owns two restaurants of similar style and price that are sited in different locations. The year-end results of the two establishments are shown in Figure 4.1.

The difference in size of the two establishments is apparent by the fact that Restaurant 2 has almost double the seating capacity and double the sales turnover compared with Restaurant 1. Also, the profit before fixed charges is greater for Restaurant 2 by over 70 per cent. As a consequence of the substantial differences in turnover and size the comparison of expenses and profit give no indication of the relative operating efficiency of the two establishments.

We can, however, effectively compare the two restaurants by using common-size profit and loss statements, shown in Figure 4.2. The sterling statements are converted into common-size statements by expressing:

- food sales and beverage sales as a percentage of total sales which shows the sales mix;
- food cost of sales and beverage cost of sales as percentages of food and beverage sales respectively;
- total gross profit as a percentage of total sales, showing the overall gross profit percentage;

FOR CARDS
OUTSIDE
THE UK,
PLEASE
AFFIX A
POSTAGE STAMP

Jo Coleman
Information Update Service
Butterworth-Heinemann
FREEPOST SCE 5435
Oxford
Oxon
OX2 8BR
UK

	Restaurant 1	Restaurant 2
Seating capacity	80	150
Sales revenue:	£	£
Food	200,000	300,000
Beverage	50,000	200,000
Total sales	250,000	500,000
Cost of sales:		
Food	65,000	117,000
Beverage	15,000	56,000
Total cost of sales	80,000	173,000
Gross profit	170,000	327,000
Controllable expenses:		
Payroll	83,000	160,000
Direct operating expenses	12,000	23,500
Marketing	8,750	22,500
Energy	8,000	17,000
Administration	10,250	20,000
Repairs and maintenance	6,250	12,500
Total controllable expenses	128,250	255,500
Profit before fixed charges	£41,750	£71,500

Figure 4.1 The Eatin Restaurant Company
Profit and loss statements for the year ended 31 December

- individual controllable expenses as a percentage of total sales;
- profit before fixed charges as a percentage of total sales.

The common-size profit and loss statements remove the influence of size and volume of business and allow us to compare the:

- proportions of food and beverage sales achieved (sales mix);
- overall gross profits to total sales;
- proportion of sales spent on each item of expense;
- profit return on total sales.

We can now compare the operating efficiency of the two restaurants using the common-size statements in Figure 4.2.

	Restaurant 1	Restaurant 2
Sales revenue:	%	%
Food	80	60
Beverage	20	40
Total sales	100	100
Cost of sales:		
Food	32.5	39
Beverage	30	28
Total cost of sales	32	34.6
Gross profit	68	65.4
Controllable expenses:		
Payroll	33.2	32.0
Direct operating expenses	4.8	4.7
Marketing	3.5	4.5
Energy	3.2	3.4
Administration	4.1	4.0
Repairs and maintenance	2.5	2.5
	51.3	51.1
Profit before fixed charges	16.7	14.3

Figure 4.2 The Eatin Restaurant Company
Common-size profit and loss statements for the year ended 31 December

In the cost of sales section of the statements the markedly lower food cost percentage in Restaurant 1 could suggest:

- better control over food purchasing;
- a better control over food usage (wastage);
- a more profitable sales mix of menu items.

The opposite is true with beverages as Restaurant 1 has a higher beverage cost of sales percentage. Thus, as a result of its higher proportion of food to beverage sales and lower food cost, Restaurant 1 has achieved a proportionately higher gross profit on sales.

In the controllable expenses section of the statements both restaurants' total expenses are slightly above 51 per cent. However, Restaurant 2 appears to have better control over payroll but has spent more on marketing. Overall, Restaurant

1 has achieved a higher profit before fixed charges, which seems to be due mainly to the more profitable food department.

Clearly, the above interpretation of the common-size statements is open to question because there might be other reasons for the differences between the two restaurants' results. We have addressed the more likely causes of the differences, but with additional knowledge of the company we could draw more specific conclusions. However, the important point to bear in mind is that by using common-size statements we will usually be in a better position to assess our operating efficiency because they provide a common basis for comparison, i.e. by comparing how much per pound of revenue we spend on each expense item.

Comparing results with industry studies

If we wish to compare our results on a broader basis it is possible to obtain industry studies which will give us an indication of how we are performing against industry in general. As most industry reports are presented in common-size form we need to convert our statements to the same format to make valid comparisons.

Let us assume that we operate a hotel in the provinces that has an average achieved room rate of £26.87 and we wish to compare our current results with industry averages. For the sake of simplicity we will only compare the rooms department operating efficiency, although a full comparison of the whole hotel would be conducted in a similar manner. Figure 4.3 shows our rooms department results converted to a common-size statement.

We can now refer to a hotel industry report and may find that the rooms department statistics appear as shown in Figure 4.4. As we can see, the industry extract contains a number of statistics, so which do we use as a yardstick against which to compare our rooms department results?

The Hollywood Hotel is a provincial establishment with an average achieved room rate for the year of £26.87. Referring to

	%
Room sales	100
Direct expenses:	
Payroll	23.1
Commissions	1.2
Linen, laundry etc.	7.1
Operating supplies	1.5
Other operating expenses	2.4
Total expenses	35.3
Department operating profit	64.7

Figure 4.3 The Hollywood Hotel
Rooms department
Common-size profit and loss statement for year ended 31 December

Figure 4.4 we can locate the closest average room rate in the 'Under £30' category which is the median value of £27.11. The values in the £27.11 column are selected for comparison with our hotel's results and presented as shown in Figure 4.5.

Remember that we are using the comparison to determine the operating efficiency of our hotel with similar provincial

	Average room rate		
	Total provinces median	Under £30 median	£30 and over median
Average room rate (£)	32.50	27.11	37.74
Rooms department			
percentage of room sales	%	%	%
Payroll	17.1	21.1	16.6
Commissions	1.6	1.3	2.2
Linens, laundry, etc.	5.8	6.7	4.4
Operating supplies	1.4	1.4	1.6
Other operating expenses	2.5	2.6	2.3
Total expenses	25.9	31.0	23.9
Departmental operating profit	74.1	69.1	75.1

Note: median values may not add to the totals shown.

Figure 4.4 Assumed Hotel Industry Report (extract)

	Hollywood Hotel	Hotel industry report	Absolute difference	Relative difference
	%	%	% points	%
Room sales	100.0	100.0		
Direct expenses (percentage of room sales):				
Payroll	23.1	20.1	+3.0	+14.9
Commissions	1.2	1.3	–0.1	–7.7
Linen, laundry, etc.	7.1	6.7	+0.4	+6.0
Operating supplies	1.5	1.4	+0.1	+7.1
Other operating expenses	2.4	2.6	–0.2	–7.7
	35.3	31.0	+4.3	+13.9
Department operating profit	64.7	69.1	–4.4	–6.4

Figure 4.5 Comparative analysis (rooms department)

hotels in the sample. In other words we are measuring the cost effectiveness of the hotel's rooms department.

By referring to Figure 4.5 we can see that the largest difference occurs in the rooms payroll. This expense is a full three percentage points higher than the industry average, representing almost 15 per cent more. The other expense items are insignificant compared with payroll.

What can we conclude from the comparison? It may point to a number of areas that are worth investigating. For instance, with regard to the difference in payroll we may be employing too many housekeeping staff. On the other hand we may be paying a higher rate compared with similar hotels. It could be a combination of the two elements, but whatever the case the differences should be interpreted carefully in the context of the level of service offered by the Hollywood Hotel and not simply reacted to by a cost-cutting exercise that may be inappropriate in this situation. The industry averages will give an indication of operating efficiency rather than a hotel-specific analysis. Along with budget and previous period comparisons, industry comparisons provide an additional base for monitoring progress.

5 Planning for profit

Managers in hotels and restaurants are constantly making decisions that affect profit. One of the decision-making areas crucial to all managers concerns profit planning. In this chapter we will consider how a manager can use a key analytical technique in a practical way to plan for profit, prepare annual budget projections and review day-to-day operations.

The technique is known as cost-volume-profit analysis (CVP) and is concerned with the relationship between sales, costs and profits. Paradoxically, CVP is widely written about, but all too often it is not used to its full potential in the practical hotel and restaurant situation.

In order to use the CVP technique we need to have a sound working knowledge of the particular business and access to the previous year's profit and loss statement. For illustration purposes we will apply the technique to a restaurant business, but it is equally applicable to other hotel and catering operations.

Fixed and variable costs

The first step we need to take when using CVP analysis for profit planning is to determine how the various cost items relate to revenue. Figure 5.1 provides an overview of how costs behave in relation to changes in the volume of sales.

We know that some costs of operating a restaurant are not influenced by changes in the volume of sales. These costs

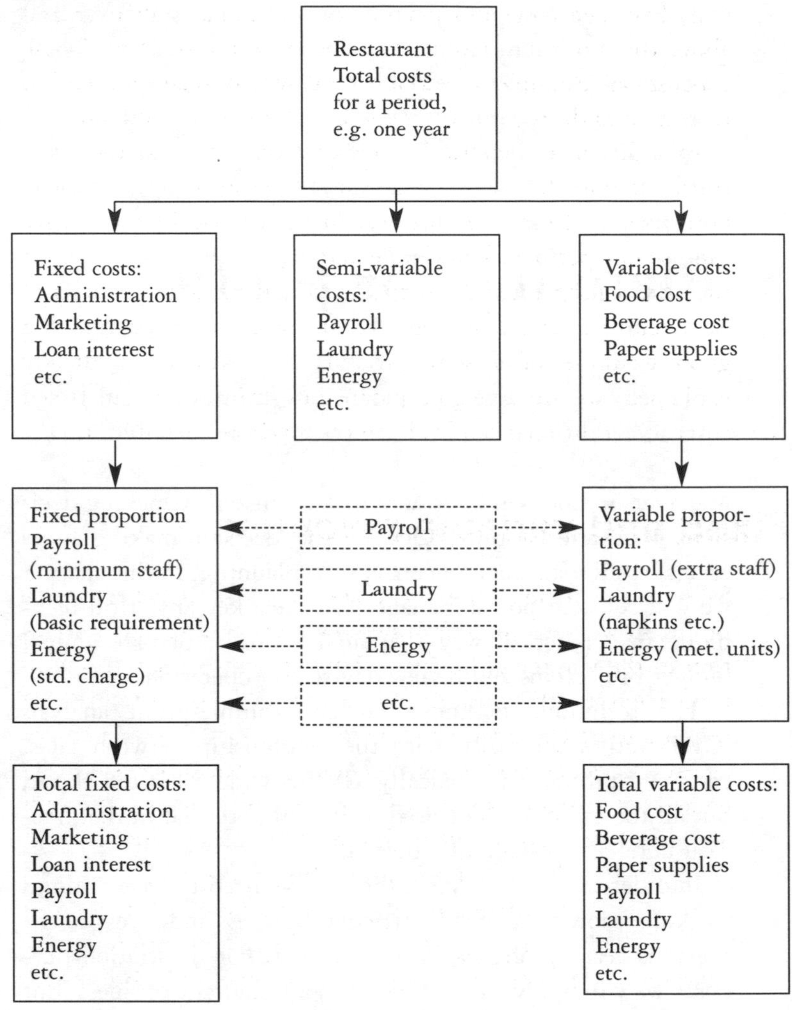

Figure 5.1 How restaurant costs behave with changes in sales volume

include loan interest, property insurance, minimum payroll and related expenses for food preparation and service staff, owner's/ management salaries, music and entertainment, and so on. These expenses are fixed costs as the amount of money is committed regardless of whether 100 or several hundred customers patronize the restaurant during a given period.

In contrast to fixed costs there are other costs that do change in proportion to the volume of sales. These costs include food cost, beverage cost, and payroll for additional staff over and above the minimum required to operate the restaurant. These expenses are examples of variable costs which in general tend to increase and decrease at the same rate as sales rise and fall.

In addition to the strictly fixed and variable costs there is a third category known as semi-variable costs which comprise both fixed and variable portions. In the practical situation we can use our personal knowledge and experience of a restaurant to make a judgement as to the fixed and variable portions of each semi-variable cost item. For instance, total payroll is a good example of a semi-variable cost which, as already explained, we are able to separate into minimum staff (fixed cost) and additional staff as business increases (variable cost).

Fixed and variable revenues

Sales is the major component associated with generating a profit, so we need to determine how revenue responds in relation to the volume of business. Thus, revenues that change in proportion to the number of customers who patronize the restaurant are classed as variable revenues, e.g. food and beverage revenues and public room rentals. On the other hand revenues that remain constant regardless of how many customers are served are classed as fixed revenues, e.g. shop space rentals, showcase rentals, club subscription dues.

As with costs, there can also be a semi-variable category for revenue. The most likely semi-variable revenue item relates to shop rentals. Sometimes an agreement is made which provides for a fixed annual rent with a variable portion based on shop sales revenue. Hence, the total rental is semi-variable although it can easily be separated into its fixed and variable portions.

Classifying revenue and expenses

Having identified the possible categories of revenue and expense items in a restaurant profit and loss statement as being wholly or partially fixed or variable, it is useful to pause and consider a summary for a typical restaurant operation, as illustrated in Figure 5.2.

The particular type and style of operation will determine the precise revenue and expense items and their degree of variability. As far as the distribution between fixed and variable revenue and expense items is concerned the person who manages the restaurant on a day-to-day basis will probably be in the best position to make the judgements. The important point to remember when analysing revenue and expenses is not to over-complicate the procedure in order to give an impression of exactness. In dealing with cost–volume–profit relationships precision is mostly an illusion. Try to keep in mind that we want our analysis to be as accurate as possible, but simple to use.

Cost–volume–profit worksheet

Now that we are able to analyse the variability of our revenues and costs we can move to the next step and prepare a CVP worksheet. This is effected by obtaining a restaurant profit and loss statement using our personal knowledge of the operation in determining the fixed and variable cost classification as outlined in Figure 5.2. For our illustration we will take the assumed results of the Cherry Tree Restaurant. The worksheet containing the distribution of fixed and variable revenue and expenses is presented in Figure 5.3.

We can see that in this case the restaurant's sales revenue is all classed as variable, whereas the expenses comprise both fixed and variable portions. The summary at the foot of the worksheet provides us with fixed and variable totals, the difference of which should equal the profit for the year. As we shall see the worksheet provides us with the basis to gain a thorough understanding of the CVP relationships of the restaurant.

Restaurant CVP calculations

From the information presented in the Cherry Tree's worksheet we can make a number of useful calculations that will be helpful in preparing annual profit projections and that will assist in assessing different possible courses of action.

However, before we can perform the various CVP calcula-

	Fixed portion	Variable portion
Sales revenue:		
Food	–	All
Beverage	–	All
Other	–	All
Public room rental	–	All
Shop space rental	Fixed annual amount	Rental portion (if any) based on percentage of sales revenue
Cost of sales:		
Food (after allowance for employee meals)	–	All
Beverage	–	All
Controllable expenses		
Payroll and related	Minimum staff for restaurant to function (manager, chef, service staff, office employees)	Additional staff as number of covers rise beyond minimum staff capacity to cope, probably 20–40% of total annual cost
Music and entertainment	All, because cost committed regardless of number of covers	–
Laundry	Amount to outfit minimum staff and cloth–up all tables initially	Uniform of additional staff plus guest napkins and table linen above fixed amount

China, glass, silver and linen	Probably 80% of total annual cost	Probably 20% of total annual cost due to breakage and damage
Paper supplies	–	All
Menus, printing, etc.	All	–
Admin and general	Almost all	–
Marketing	All, but franchise fee based on sales revenue	Franchise fee portion based upon percentage of sales revenue
Energy and utilities	Almost all (amount affected by season and decision to open more or less hours, but not affected by number of covers)	–
Repairs and maintenance	Almost all	–
Fixed charges:		
Rent	All fixed amount	Only the amount (if any) based on a percentage of sales revenue
Property insurance	All	–
Business rate	All	–
Loan interest	All	–
Depreciation	All	–
Net profit before tax	–	All

Figure 5.2 Classification of restaurant revenues and expenses in terms of fixed and variable portions

	Year 19 × 1	Classification Fixed	Variable	Explanation
	£	£	£	
Sales revenue:				
Food	200,000	–	200,000	
Beverage	150,000	–	150,000	
Gift items	40,000	–	40,000	
Total	390,000			
Cost of sales:				
Food	80,000	–	80,000	
Beverage	70,000	–	70,000	
Gift items	20,000	–	20,000	
Total	170,000			
Gross Profit	220,000			
Other income	30,000	–	30,000	Banquet/meeting room rentals
Total Income	250,000	–		

	£	£	£	
Controllable expenses:				
Payroll	90,000	60,000	30,000	Extra staff 331/3 of total payroll
Laundry	5,300	2,000	3,300	
China, glass etc.	12,000	10,000	2,000	
Paper supplies	2,500	–	2,500	
Menus and printing	2,000	2,000	–	
Admin and general	14,000	14,000	–	
Marketing	16,000	9,000	7,000	Franchise fee 2% Food and bev. sales
Repairs and Maint	8,500	8,500	–	
Energy	9,000	7,500	1,500	
Total	159,300			
Profit before fixed charges	90,700			
Fixed charges:				
Rent	16,500	6,000	10,500	Fixed £6,000 plus 3% of food and bev. sales
Business rate and insurance	8,000	8,000	–	
Loan interest	15,000	15,000	–	
Depreciation	14,000	14,000	–	
Total	53,500			
Profit for year	£37,200			

Summary

Revenue			*Expenses*		
	Fixed	Variable		Fixed	Variable
	£	£		£	£
Food sales	–	200,000	Food cost	–	80,000
Beverage sales	–	150,000	Beverage cost	–	70,000
Gift items sales	–	40,000	Gift items cost	–	20,000
Banquet/meeting	–		Controllable expenses	113,000	46,300
Room rentals	–	30,000	Fixed charges	43,000	10,500
	–	420,000		156,000	226,800

Total revenue £420,000–Total expenses £382,800 = Profit £37,200

Figure 5.3 Cost–volume–profit worksheet. The Cherry Tree Restaurant profit and loss statement for year ended 31 December 19×1

tions we need to determine three pieces of information from the worksheet summary in Figure 5.3.

1 Variable cost percentage
This figure is obtained by dividing variable costs by sales revenue and expressing the result as a percentage, as follows:

$$\text{VC\%} = \frac{\text{Variable costs}}{\text{Sales revenue}} = \frac{£226{,}800}{£420{,}000} = 54 \text{ per cent}$$

2 Contribution margin percentage
This is determined by subtracting variable costs from sales revenue, dividing the result by sales revenue and expressing it as a percentage, as follows:

$$\text{CM\%} = \frac{(\text{Sales revenue} - \text{variable costs})}{\text{Sales revenue}} = \frac{£420{,}000 - £226{,}800}{£420{,}000} = 46 \text{ per cent}$$

or simply by subtracting the variable cost percentage from 100 per cent i.e. CM% = 100% – 54% = 46%

3 Fixed costs
This figure is obtained directly from the worksheet summary, i.e. fixed costs = £156,000.

Break-even sales volume

A business achieves break-even when total revenues are equal to total costs. Although break-even may not be an end objective in itself, it is an important intermediate point that must be reached prior to making a profit. Thus, the psychological significance that a knowledge of the break-even point represents to operators and managers should not be disregarded in the profit planning process.

If each £1 of sales revenue leaves £0.46 after recouping variable costs of £0.54 how much sales revenue is required to recover fixed costs of £156,000?

$$\text{Break-even sales volume} = \frac{\text{Fixed costs}}{\text{Contribution margin \%}}$$
$$= £156{,}000/0.46$$
$$= £336{,}130$$

Thus, the break-even figure informs us that £339,130 of sales revenue generates £156,000 worth of contribution margin, i.e. (£339,130 × 0.46) which is sufficient to pay for our fixed costs (break-even point), and thereafter each £1 of sales revenue contributes £0.46 towards profit for the period.

Sales volume for a target profit

The same principle is applied here as for break-even sales volume, i.e. if each pound of sales revenue generates £0.46 after accounting for variable costs, how much sales revenue is required to cover fixed costs of £156,000 and generate our restaurant's profit of £37,200? The rule is simply to treat profit as a fixed cost, as follows:

$$\text{Sales volume for target profit} = \frac{(\text{Fixed costs} + \text{target profit})}{\text{Contribution margin \%}}$$
$$= \frac{(£156{,}000 + £37{,}200)}{0.46}$$
$$= £420{,}000$$

If we refer to Figure 5.3 we can confirm that the £420,000 appears in the summary at the foot of the worksheet.

Sales volume to make up a loss

Treat the loss as a fixed cost. If we assume our restaurant made a loss of £5,000 the calculation is as follows:

$$\text{Sales volume to recover a loss} = \frac{\text{Loss}}{\text{Contribution margin \%}} = \frac{\pounds5{,}000}{0.46} = \pounds10{,}870$$

Cost–volume–profit graph

In order to obtain additional insights into the sales cost and profit relationships of a business we need to prepare a CVP graph. Again, using the results of the Cherry Tree Restaurant we can prepare a CVP graph as illustrated in Figure 5.4.

A CVP graph provides us with a visual picture of how costs relate to changes in the volume of business. The graph also enables us to identify the following items:

- fixed, variable and total costs, and total revenue;
- break-even in sales volume;
- profits or losses above and below target sales within a relevant range.

The CVP graph also enables us to gain an impression of the

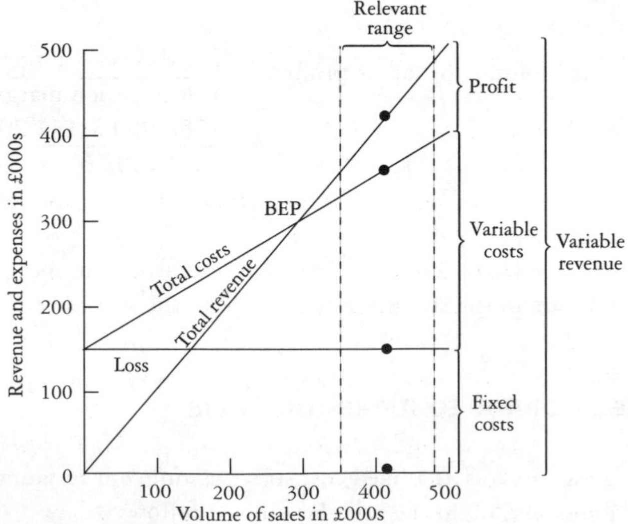

Figure 5.4 The Cherry Tree Restaurant cost–volume–profit graph

cost structure of a business, i.e. the proportion of fixed costs to total costs. The higher the proportion of fixed costs to total costs the more dramatic the effect on profit of changes in the level of demand.

To be able to make practical use of CVP formulas and graphs we need to satisfy two basic assumptions:

- Revenues and costs can be realistically separated into the fixed and variable categories.
- Revenues and costs respond in a linear, or straightline, function.

Because it is not possible to be absolutely sure that both assumptions have been satisfied we can limit our CVP analysis by using a relevant range on the graph and for the formula computations. Experience suggests that this range is generally accurate 15–20 per cent above and below the estimated level at which we have accurate data.

Constructing a cost–volume–profit graph

In Figure 5.3 the Cherry Tree Restaurant profit and loss statement is extended into a worksheet which distributes revenues and expenses in the fixed and variable categories. This provides the basis for constructing the CVP graph.

The actual sales volume is £420,000 so we will scale both the horizontal and vertical axis to £500,000 to allow for the relevant range. The £420,000 is indicated on the horizontal line and each revenue and expense item is plotted directly above that point. The £156,000 fixed cost is plotted first and we draw a line parallel to the horizontal axis. Next, we plot £382,800 total cost and draw a line to the fixed cost intersection at zero sales volume. The variable costs form the wedge between total cost and fixed cost. Finally, we plot the £420,000 sales revenue and draw a line down to zero sales volume where the horizontal and vertical axes meet. At £420,000 sales volume, the grid space between the total revenue and total cost lines indicate the Cherry Tree's profit is around the £37,200 given in the worksheet; the restaurant's break-even volume is around the £339,130 computed earlier and is determined at the point at which total revenue equals total cost.

If we establish the relevant range at (say) 15 per cent above or below the present sales level of £420,000 we would regard the graph's accuracy as being between £357,000 and £483,000, indicated in Figure 5.4. Thus, for profit planning purposes we can determine our profits (or losses) at any level of volume between these two figures and be reasonably assured of their accuracy (we will see later, in Chapter 10, how simply and effectively CVP worksheets, computations and graphs can be incorporated in a computer spreadsheet model).

Restaurant CVP calculations for decision making

Having explored the practicalities of CVP analysis we can now look at an example of how the technique can help us in a decision-making situation. We will assume the situation where a restaurant has made a loss during the month, presented in Figure 5.5. Let us consider some of the alternative courses of action that will return the Rainbow Restaurant to a break-even position.

Our first step is to determine all variable costs and express each one as a percentage of the appropriate sales revenue, indicated in Figure 5.5.

1 *Raise only food prices to break-even, with no change in sales volume.*
Solution: increase food prices by £1,800 or 15 per cent

i.e. $\frac{£1,800}{£12,000} = 15$ per cent

2 *Raise all prices to break-even, with no change in sales volume.*
Solution: increase all prices by £1,800 or 9 per cent

i.e. $\frac{£1,800}{£20,000} = 9$ per cent

Sales revenue	£	
Food	12,000	60% of total sales
Beverage	6,000	30% of total sales
Other	2,000	10% of total sales
Total revenue	20,000	100% of total sales
Cost of sales		
Food	5,400	45% of food sales
Beverage	2,100	35% of bev. sales
Other	500	25% of other sales
Total cost of sales	8,000	40% of total sales
Gross profit	12,000	
Operating expenses (variable)	3,000	15% of total sales
Operating expenses (fixed)	6,800	
Fixed charges (fixed)	4,000	
Total	13,800	
Net profit (loss) for the month	(1,800)	

Figure 5.5 The Rainbow Restaurant
Profit statement for the month ended 31 January

3 *Increase only food sales volume to break-even.*

Solution: VC = 45 per cent (food cost) + 15 per cent (operating expenses)
= 60 per cent

CM = 100 – 60 per cent
= 40 per cent

$$\text{Additional food sales volume} = \frac{\text{Loss}}{\text{CM\%}}$$

= £1,800/0.4

= £4,500

Similar principle if only beverage or other sales volume are increased

4 *Increase all sales volume in the present sales mix to break-even.*
Solution: VC = 40 per cent (food, beverage and other sales to total sales) + 15 per cent (operating expenses)
= 55 per cent
CM = 100 – 55 per cent
= 45 per cent
Additional total sales volume = Loss/CM %
= £1,800/0.45
= £4,000

5 *Increase only beverage and other sales volume in the proportions 60 per cent beverage and 40 per cent other sales to break-even.*
Solution: Bev. VC = 35 per cent (beverage cost) + 15 per cent (operating expenses)
= 50 per cent
CM = 100 – 50 per cent
= 50 per cent
Other VC = 25 per cent (other cost) + 15 per cent (operating expenses)
= 40 per cent
CM = 100 – 40 per cent
= 60 per cent

	(CM)		(SM)		
Beverage	0.5	×	0.6	=	0.3
Other	0.6	×	0.4	=	0.24
					0.54

Average beverage and other sales = $\frac{£1,800}{0.54}$
= £3,334

Similar principle if other sales mix combinations are used.

6 *Reduce fixed operating expenses to break-even.*
Solution: decrease fixed operating expenses by £1,800

7 *Reduce food cost percentage to break-even.*
Solution: new food cost percentage = $\frac{(\text{Food cost} - \text{loss})}{\text{Food sales}}$
= $\frac{(£5,400 - £1,800)}{£12,000}$
= 30 per cent

8 *Increase food sales volume by 10 per cent and reduce food cost percentage to break-even.*

Solution: new food cost percentage $= \dfrac{(£5,400 + £540 - £1,320^*)}{(£12,000 + £1,200)}$

$= 35$ per cent

*Extra: food sales		£1,200	(£12,000 × 10 per cent)
food cost	£540		(£1,200 × 45 per cent)
operating expenses	180	720	(£ 1,200 × 15 per cent)
Additional profit		480	
Loss to make-up		1,800	
Reduction in food cost required		£1,320	

The extra food sales, after accounting for food cost, at the present food cost percentage, and operating expenses yields an additional profit of £480. This leaves £1,320 to be made up from the food cost reduction on the new £13,200 food sales volume resulting in a food cost of 35 per cent. Hence, if a 10 per cent increase in food sales volume is achieved and food cost is reduced to 35 per cent, the restaurant will break even.

Supposing we had the situation where the Rainbow Restaurant wished to eliminate its £1,800 loss and generate a profit of £2,000. Simply treat the desired profit as a fixed cost and add it to the loss and proceed through the eight courses of action illustrated above. For example, take the third alternative:

Increase only food sales volume to recover a loss and generate profit.

Solution: food sales volume increase $= \dfrac{(\text{Loss} + \text{desired profit})}{\text{CM\%}}$

$= (£1,800 + £2,000)/0.4$

$= £9,500$

If we are currently operating a restaurant at a profit and wish to increase the profit by £3,500, treat the additional profit as a fixed cost and proceed through the courses of action adopting the formula as appropriate. For example, take alternative (3) again:

Increase food sales volume to produce an additional profit.

$$\text{Solution: food sales volume increase} = \frac{\text{Additional profit}}{\text{CM\%)}}$$

$$= \frac{£3{,}500}{0.4}$$

$$= £8{,}750$$

We have considered some possible courses of action that a manager can take in order to improve an operating situation, but there are many other combinations to choose from. Whatever the decision chosen we should be able to adapt the CVP formulas and compute the results.

Hotel CVP calculations

Until now we have considered CVP analysis in the context of restaurants, but the techniques are equally applicable to hotels. In addition to expressing CVP relationships relating to price, volume, sales mix and cost changes in financial terms presented earlier, it is particularly useful to determine room occupancy levels necessary to break-even and achieve specific profit targets. This provides managers with an operational expression of what is required to achieve given targets – an important aspect as financial goals need to be translated into operational terms in order to determine the actual volumes of products and services to be sold.

Hotel break-even occupancy (Method 1)

Using the information given in Figure 5.6 a method of determining hotel 'break-even room occupancy' is illustrated.

To determine break-even room occupancy, first total sales revenue of £200,000 from the profit and loss statement (Figure 5.6) and total variable costs from the cost analysis (Figure 5.7)

	Hotel Profit and Loss Statement	Cost Behaviour Analysis	
		Fixed	Varaiable
	£		
Total sales revenue	200,000		
Less: Direct expenses:			
Cost of sales	30,000	–	100%
Payroll	36,000	70%	30%
Other	16,000	40%	60%
	82,000		
Gross operating income	118,000		
Less: Undistributed Operating expenses	46,000	80%	20%
Gross operating profit	72,000		
Less: Fixed charges	50,000	100%	–
Net profit before tax	22,000		

The hotel has 100 rooms and achieved 70 per cent room occupancy during May

Figure 5.6 The Granville Hotel
Summarized profit statement for the month ended 31 may

	Total Costs	Fixed Costs	Variable Costs
	£	£	£
Direct expenses:			
Cost of sales	30,000	–	30,000
Payroll	36,000	25,200	10,800
Other	16,000	6,400	9,600
Indirect expenses:			
UOE	46,000	36,800	9,200
Fixed charges	50,000	50,000	–
Total	178,000	118,400	59,600

Figure 5.7 The Granville Hotel
Distribution of fixed and variable costs

are ascertained in order to determine the weighted contribution margin (WCM), as follows:

Total sales revenue	£200,000
Less: VC	59,600
WCM	140,400

The total hotel WCM of £140,400 is then divided by the number of rooms occupied during the month (31days × 100 rooms available × 70 per cent occupancy = 2,170 rooms) to give the WCM per room occupied (£64.70). The total hotel fixed costs (£118,400) are then divided by the WCM per room occupied and the result expressed as a percentage of rooms available, as follows:

Room occupancy
to break-even =

$$\frac{\text{Fixed costs}}{\text{WCM per room}} = \frac{£118{,}400}{£64{,}70} = 1{,}830 \text{ rooms}$$

$$\frac{\text{Rooms occupied}}{\text{Rooms available}} = \frac{1{,}830 \times 100}{3{,}100} = 59\%$$

Furthermore, to determine the level of room occupancy to achieve the £22,000 net profit before tax shown in the profit and loss statement (Figure 5.6), the calculation is as follows:

Room occupancy
for target profit =

$$\frac{\text{Fixed costs + net profit}}{\text{WCM per room}} = \frac{£118{,}400 + £22{,}000}{£64.70}$$

$$= 2{,}170 \text{ rooms}$$

$$\frac{\text{Rooms occupied}}{\text{Rooms available}} = \frac{2{,}170 \times 100}{3{,}100} = 70\%$$

Note: With this method the WCM per room occupied of £64.70 combines the CM from rooms, food and beverage, and minor operated department sales revenue to give the average total CM in relation to each room occupied.

Hence, the ability to analyse the distribution of fixed and variable costs in the profit statement facilitates the calculation and review of occupancy levels required to attain break-even and various profit scenarios.

Hotel break-even occupancy (Method 2)

An alternative more simplified method of determining break-even and profit and loss levels is available. This approach modifies the analysis of cost behaviour stage by making the general assumption that *all* undistributed operating expenses and fixed charges are fixed costs and that *all* direct operated department expenses are variable costs, thus resulting in the gross operating income (GOI) substituting for the traditional contribution margin, as follows:

Total sales revenue	£200,000
Less: Direct expenses	82,000
GOI	118,000

The total weighted gross operating income (WGOI) of £118,000 is then divided by the 2170 rooms occupied during the month to give the WGOI per room occupied (54.38). The total (assumed) hotel fixed costs of £96,000 are then divided by the WGOI per room occupied and the result expressed as a percentage of rooms available, as follows:

Room occupancy
to break-even =

$$\frac{\text{Fixed costs}}{\text{WGOI per room}} \quad \frac{£96{,}000}{£54.38} = 1766 \text{ rooms}$$

$$\frac{\text{Rooms occupied}}{\text{Rooms available}} \quad \frac{1766 \times 100}{3{,}100} = 57\%$$

Furthermore, to determine the level of room occupancy to achieve the £22,000 net profit before tax in the profit and loss statement (Figure 5.6), the calculation is as follows:

Room occupancy
for target profit

$$\frac{\text{Fixed costs + net profit}}{\text{WGOI per room}} \quad \frac{£96{,}000 + £22{,}000}{£54.38} = 2170$$

$$\frac{\text{Rooms occupied}}{\text{Rooms available}} \quad \frac{2{,}170 \times 100}{3{,}100} = 70\%$$

Note: Similarly in principle to Method 1, the WGOI per room occupied of £54.38 combines the GOI from rooms, food and beverage, and minor operated department sales revenue to give the average total GOI in relation to each room occupied.

Comparison of the above two methods of calculating room occupancy for break-even and profit indicates that, whilst the room occupancy required to achieve the profit target of £22,000 is similar at 70 per cent occupancy, the occupancy at break-even is higher under Method 1. The reason for this is that in the case of the Granville Hotel example the proportion of fixed costs to total costs under Method 1 is higher than under Method 2. If we assume the more detailed cost analysis carried out under Method 1 is more representative of the relationship between the hotel's volume of business and related cost behaviour then it becomes clear that the break-even room occupancy of 59 per cent under Method 1 provides a more accurate result than under Method 2, which understates occupancy at 57 per cent.

Whilst in the case of the Granville Hotel the 2 per cent difference in room occupancy occurring from the two methods is negligible, in other cases the differences may prove to be far greater and, therefore, result in undermining the validity of Method 2. However, the important point to remember is that in a given scenario, if the proportion of fixed costs are understated the resulting break-even occupancy threshold will also be understated and that the greater the discrepancy the more inaccurate the analysis becomes. Both methods are useful aids to decision-making, but the choice of method selected should take account of the particular situation and the degree of accuracy required.

As we have tried to show here, cost–volume–profit analysis is a powerful technique that can be of immense practical use to managers involved in profit planning decisions. It can help us to understand the underlying sales, cost, profit relationships of a business and, although it cannot solve operational problems, it can assist us in qualifying our profit position and formulating possible courses of action.

6 Pricing hotel and restaurant services

As we discussed at the outset, the majority of products and services produced and sold in the hotel and catering industry are derived from the provision of rooms, food and beverages. Pricing these facilities requires a sound knowledge of the financial factors that surround them and of the market. For instance, we need to be aware of customer perception and expectation of product prices in our market segment and become familiar with what our competitors are charging for similar items. We should also be aware of the costs incurred in providing our products and services, and these include profit, which as far as our business is concerned is also a cost.

In this chapter we will focus our attention on the more practical approaches to hotel and restaurant pricing decisions. We will also endeavour to show how to develop an overall pricing policy for a business. First of all, however, it is worthwhile for us briefly to consider the fundamental methods of pricing any kind of item.

General pricing methods

Essentially, there are three basic ways of pricing products and services, with numerous variations of each:

- cost-plus;
- contribution margin;
- going rate.

Cost-plus pricing

With this method selling prices are set at a level to recover all costs, which includes direct costs, a share of the unallocated costs (overheads), plus a predetermined profit. This can be expressed as a simple formula, as follows:

Total costs + profit = selling price

The 'plus' or profit portion is usually related to a target rate of return on owners' capital invested.

The problem with this method of pricing is the assumption that the correct, and therefore acceptable, price to the consumer is the sum of all our costs plus a predetermined profit return. It is a product rather than market-related method which if used mechanistically will disregard the consumer, and ignore competition.

The general argument for using cost-plus pricing is that it is a safer way of pricing products because it seeks to cover all costs and ensure long-term profitability.

Contribution margin pricing

Contribution margin pricing is also known as marginal cost pricing. This pricing approach focuses on maximizing contribution margins to recover fixed costs and generate a profit. The method requires us to analyse costs into their fixed and variable categories (explained in Chapter 5).

Fixed costs are treated as period costs and are not absorbed into the products or services. Prices are set using marginal cost (variable cost per unit) as the floor and what the customer will bear as the ceiling. It therefore requires a practical knowledge of cost–volume–profit analysis which is perhaps why it is regarded as a less safe form of pricing.

The method facilitates a flexible pricing policy because it allows a greater range of price discretion. This is due to the fact that we price from the variable cost as opposed to the total cost when using cost-plus pricing.

Contribution margin pricing tends to be used for short-term (tactical) pricing decisions. The danger of using it for long-term pricing decisions is that there is an underlying fear that the total contributions generated may not be sufficient to recover the period fixed costs and return a profit. However, the method does take account of both the market and the cost of providing facilities.

Going rate pricing

This method of pricing, also known as market pricing, is the opposite of cost-plus pricing as it emphasizes the market as opposed to the cost. In this case prices are set in relation to the perceived market need and costs are tailored accordingly.

If going rate pricing is to be used we must be prepared to manage our costs in order to ensure that a profit is achieved. This is an easier task in manufacturing concerns because they usually contain a high proportion of variable costs which offer considerable opportunity for cost manipulation. On the other hand hotels and restaurants normally contain a low proportion of variable costs which provide less opportunity for cost adjustment.

Where going rate is used rigidly there is a danger of the costs being treated on a piecemeal basis in order to force them to a predetermined level. This may undermine the quality and consistency of the products and services which in turn would lead to a drop in demand.

What pricing method?

While the demands of the consumer must always be uppermost in our minds we cannot neglect our responsibilities to owners and investors. On the one hand, we need to develop a price structure that is acceptable to the market, and on the other we must try to ensure the proprietors and shareholders receive an adequate return on their investment. This is often a difficult balance to achieve, but as we will see it is possible to do so if we take a pragmatic approach and draw on the benefits of all three pricing methods.

Restaurant pricing

The first step is to determine an average spend for our restaurant that will provide an adequate return on investors' capital. For this we will use the cost-plus rate of return pricing method outlined earlier. It is sometimes referred to as the 'bottom up' approach to pricing because we start with the required profit return on investment, which is the 'bottom line' in terms of a profit and loss statement, and work our way 'up' estimating the various cost items, including profit, in order to arrive at food revenue.

Let us take an example using the assumed figures of the Winterburn Restaurant, an 80-seater establishment with projections for next year as presented in Figure 6.1.

We can summarize the costs and profit contained in Figure 6.1.

We know the direct operating costs are 75 per cent of revenue (10% + 25% + 40%), therefore, the other costs and profit of £106,000 must represent 25 per cent of revenue. With this information we are able to calculate the projected revenue as below:

$$\text{Projected revenue} = \frac{\pounds 106{,}000}{25\%} = \pounds 424{,}000$$

Providing the Winterburn Restaurant achieves the projected revenue and costs it will return a profit after tax of 10 per cent on owners' capital i.e. £21,000 as shown in Figure 6.2.

Net profit after tax	£21,000
Tax	£9,000
Overheads	£76,000
Total	£106,000

Net profit required after tax	10% of owner's equity of £210,000 = £21,000
Tax rate	30% on net profit before tax (21,000 ÷ 70) × 30 = £9,000

Overheads:		
Depreciation	£11,000	Total = £76,000
Rent	£24,200	
Business rate	£12,200	
Administration	£10,800	
Energy and repairs	£9,300	
Marketing	£8,500	

Direct operating expenses:			
Other (laundry etc.)	10%	of revenue	Total = 75 per cent
Payroll	25%		
Food cost	40%		

Figure 6.1 The Winterburn Restaurant. Projections for next year

	£	
Sales revenue	424,000	← 100%
Direct operating expenses	318,000	← 75%
	106,000	
Overheads	76,000	← 25%
Net profit before tax	30,000	
Tax 30% of profit	9,000	← 25%
Net profit after tax	21,000	← 25%

Figure 6.2 The Winterburn Restaurant. Projected profit statement for next year

Average spend

Having determined the projected annual food revenue we can now calculate the restaurant's average spend, which is the next step to pricing the menu items.

The basic formula is as follows:

$$\text{Average spend} = \frac{\text{Annual food revenue}}{\text{Annual number of food covers}}$$

In order to ascertain the annual number of food covers sold we need to know seating capacity (80 seats), the anticipated seat turnover (two times per day) and the number of days per year the restaurant is open (five days × 52 weeks = 260 days per year):

$$\text{Average spend} = \frac{\text{Annual food revenue}}{\text{Number of seats} \times \text{daily turnover} \times \text{days per year}}$$

$$= \frac{£424{,}000}{80 \times 2 \times 260}$$

$$= \frac{£424{,}000}{41{,}600}$$

$$= £10.19$$

The average spend does not indicate what individual customers will spend, nor does it tell us the menu prices; it simply informs us what customers should be spending on average if we are to achieve our profit objective. If, other things remaining constant, the average spend begins to slide we will need to take action to rectify the situation or accept a shortfall in profit.

The average spend has an important part to play in developing a menu pricing policy because it provides us with an indication of what our restaurant pricing structure should be.

Average spend per meal period

The next step towards developing a menu pricing policy is to determine the average spend per meal period. Even if the same menu is offered for lunch and dinner periods it is useful to determine each meal period spend. The reason for this is that we would not normally anticipate the same average spend, or indeed, the same average seat turnover, for each period. People display different eating habits between daytime and evening. They tend to take longer over a meal in the evening, compared with lunchtimes, choosing more items and often from the higher priced selections. If eating patterns are significantly different between meal periods they will affect seat turnover and average spend, and we need to know by how much so we can take the appropriate action.

We can determine the average spend per meal period by estimating the proportion of total annual revenue for each period and the associated seat turnovers. If the restaurant is an existing business we can refer to past records. Assuming the Winterburn Restaurant is a lunch and dinner establishment where we expect lunch to account for 40 per cent of revenue with a seat turnover of 1.2, and dinner to account for 60 per cent of revenue with a seat turnover of 0.8, we can calculate the average spend per meal period as follows:

$$\text{Average spend per meal period} = \frac{\text{Meal period \% of annual revenue} \times \text{Annual revenue}}{\text{Number of seats} \times \text{daily turnover} \times \text{days per year}}$$

$$\text{Average spend for lunch period} = \frac{40\% \times £424{,}000}{80 \times 1.2 \times 260} = \frac{£169{,}600}{24{,}960} = £6.80$$

$$\text{Average spend for dinner period} = \frac{60\% \times £424{,}000}{80 \times 0.8 \times 260} = \frac{£254{,}400}{16{,}640} = £15.29$$

So, although the overall average spend for the restaurant is £10.19 (calculated earlier) we can see that the meal period average spends are significantly different at lunch £6.80, and dinner £15.29. We can verify these figures as follows:

Lunch	80 × 1.2 × 260 × £6.80 =	£169,728
Dinner	80 × 0.8 × 260 × £15.29 =	£254,426
Total revenue		£424,154

The projected revenue is £424,000, therefore the difference is due to rounding. Note also that as with the overall average spend the meal period average spends do not indicate the menu prices but what the average spend should be to achieve our profit target.

Pricing menu items

The final step in developing a restaurant pricing policy is to price the individual menu items. In doing this we should remember that during the coming year we must achieve an overall gross profit percentage of 60 per cent (after recovering food cost of 40 per cent) in order to generate sufficient cash gross profit to cover all our other costs and net profit (see Figure 6.2).

In theory we could apply a constant gross profit percentage of 60 per cent to each menu item. Clearly, this will normally give prices which are either too high or too low because ingredient costs vary considerably from item to item. This will usually be out of line with competitors and unacceptable to customers.

In order to harmonize our menu prices we need to determine the food cost and assign an appropriate selling price to each item. Some items will have a gross profit percentage higher than 60 per cent and some will be lower. We then need to determine the sales mix of the whole menu by estimating the number of each item we expect to sell. Remember some customers may choose one or two items while others may select two or three items. Food cost and gross profit should be subject to close control, especially initially, as for instance we may find we are achieving revenue levels but not generating sufficient gross profit to cover our other costs. This may call for a price review, cost adjustment or substitution of one menu item for another that is more profitable. It's a delicate balancing act, but one we must perform if our restaurant is to succeed.

A practical way to carry out a check to see if we will generate sufficient gross profit to recover our other costs and profit is as follows.

Determine the anticipated revenue sales mix by multiplying the estimated number of each menu item by its proposed selling price (assume a two week period):

Menu item	Estimated items sold		Selling price £	Total revenue £	Sales mix %	
1	800	×	2.50 =	2,000	10	
2	1,600	×	5.00 =	8,000	40	
3	1,000	×	6.00 =	6,000	30	
4	500	×	8.00 =	4,000	20	
	3,900			20,000	100	per cent

Now, multiply each menu item sales mix percentage by a predetermined gross profit percentage to give a weighted gross profit percentage:

Menu item	Sales mix %		Gross profit %		Weighted gross profit %	
1	10	×	75	=	7.5	
2	40	×	55	=	22	
3	30	×	70	=	21	
4	20	×	50	=	10	
					60.5	per cent

Note that this gives an overall (weighted) gross profit of 60.5 per cent which is just above the 60 per cent target gross profit percentage required for the Winterburn Restaurant. If the gross profit percentage had turned out significantly lower than our required 60 per cent we would need carefully to adjust selling price and food costs in order to bring it back into line.

As we have already said it is a juggling act which nevertheless has to be done.

Note also that, assuming each customer consumes two menu items, then 1,950 covers would be sold (3,900 ÷ 2), generating £20,000 revenue. Our average spend for the two-week example period would be as follows:

$$\text{Average spend} = \frac{\pounds 20{,}000}{1{,}950 \text{ covers}} = \pounds 10.26$$

This is satisfactory because it is slightly above the projected average spend of £10.19. Also, our average seat turnover for the period is 2.4 calculated by (1,950 ÷ 10 days) ÷ 80 seats, which is also up on the anticipated two times in our projections.

Remember in order to achieve our target rate of return on owners' capital invested we must maintain the projected level of the following components:

- average spend;
- seat turnover;
- gross profit.

If one of these components begins to slide we will need to take corrective measures to compensate by improving one or both of the other two.

Note: A similar approach can be used for pricing beverages as has been described here for menu pricing.

Hotel room pricing

As with restaurant pricing, the first step we need to take is to determine an average room rate that will provide an acceptable return on owners' capital.

To determine the average room rate we will use the Hubbart Formula. As we will see, this is simply the rate of return variation of the cost-plus pricing method outlined earlier. It too is sometimes referred to as the 'bottom-up' approach to pricing because, as before, we start with the required profit return on investment and work our way 'up' estimating all the various cost and profit items, with the exception of rooms revenue. Let us take an example using the assumed figures of the Strand Hotel, a 60-room property with projections for the next year as presented in Figure 6.3. Applying the Hubbart Formula the average room rate is calculated as illustrated in Figure 6.4. Note, the rooms revenue is determined by totalling all projected costs, including profit, that are to be recovered and deducting any department profit contributions excluding rooms. Rooms revenue is then divided by the projected number of rooms sold to arrive at the average room rate of £50.

The £50 is only an average rate which may not necessarily be the actual rate for any one room. It is, however, an important figure because it acts as a guide for pricing single and double occupancy, and different sizes and types of room. In the end we must actually achieve a minimum overall average room rate of £50, other factors remaining constant, if we are to recover our costs and produce the required profit.

Single and double room rates

We can demonstrate how to calculate single and double room rates partly by drawing on the Strand Hotel information. The first step is to determine the double occupancy percentage. We know the hotel's projected occupancy is 70 per cent. If the projected number of guest nights for the coming year is 22,995 we can calculate the double occupancy as shown in Figure 6.3.

Total guest nights during year	22,995
Less: number of rooms sold	15,330
Number of rooms double occupied	7,665

$$\text{Double occupancy percentage} = \frac{\text{Rooms double occupied}}{\text{Rooms sold}}$$

$$= \frac{7{,}665}{15{,}330} = 50 \text{ per cent}$$

Now, having determined our double occupancy rate the second step is to calculate our single and double room rates. We will assume a differential rate of £10.

Net profit required after tax — 10% on owners' equity of £1,260,000 = £126,000

Tax rate — 30% on net profit before tax = (£126,000 ÷ 70) × 30 = £54,000

Fixed charges:

Depreciation	£45,000	
Loan interest	12% on £600,000 loan = £72,000	Total = £161,000
Business rate	£44,000	

Undistributed operating expenses:

Energy	£53,000	
Property repairs	£55,000	
Marketing	£36,000	
Administration	£98,000	Total = £242,000

Departmental profits:

Food and beverage	£61,000	after deducting cost of sales, payroll and expenses	Total = £66,500
Telephone	£5,500		

Rooms department direct costs — £250,000 payroll and other expenses

Number of rooms to be sold — 60 × 70% × 365 days = 15,330 rooms

Figure 6.3 The Strand Hotel. Projections for next year

On a typical night during the year we will expect to sell 42 rooms (60 rooms × 70 per cent occupancy). Of these 21 rooms (50 per cent) will be double occupancy and 21 rooms (50 per cent) will be single occupancy. Furthermore, based on our previously calculated average room rate of £50 we would expect to generate £2,100 (42 rooms × £50).

To determine the single and double room rates we need to solve a simple equation where x is the single occupancy rate, as follows:

Profit after tax	126,000
Tax	54,000
Fixed charges	161,000
Undistributed operating expenses	242,000
Rooms department direct cost	250,000
	833,000
Food and beverage, and telephone departments' profits	66,500
Rooms revenue required	£766,500
Number of rooms to be sold	15,330

$$\text{Projected average room rate} = \frac{\text{Rooms revenue}}{\text{Rooms to be sold}}$$

$$= \frac{£766{,}500}{15{,}330} = \underline{£50}$$

Figure 6.4 The Strand Hotel. Projected average room rate for next year

$$
\begin{aligned}
21x + 21\,(x + £10) &= £2{,}100 \\
21x + 21x + £210 &= £2{,}100 \\
42x &= £2{,}100 - £210 \\
42x &= £1{,}890 \\
x &= \frac{£1{,}890}{42} \\
x &= 45
\end{aligned}
$$

Thus, our single rate is £45 and our double rate is £55 (£45 + £10). We can check the ratios as follows:

		£
21 singles	× £45 =	945
21 doubles	× £55 =	1,155
42 rooms	× £50 =	2,100

If our other assumptions for the Strand Hotel prove to be valid we would expect the profit return on investment to be achieved.

Developing an overall pricing policy

There is no single approach to formulating an overall hotel or restaurant pricing policy that will be applicable to every situation. Neither is there any one pricing method that can be applied exclusively, disregarding all others. However, in many cases we can develop an effective pricing policy in practice by using a two-tier approach that draws on all three of the pricing methods explained earlier. In this way we can normally overcome the conflicts inherent in each method and evolve a practical policy that satisfies customers' demands and owners' requirements. Let us therefore consider the two-tier approach which is generally applicable to a wide range of establishments.

Primary pricing decisions

In order to determine our restaurant and room prices we computed the average spend per cover and the average room rate. We did this so as to get some idea of the overall figure required to recover costs and achieve a reasonable profit return on investment. We then proceeded to price our menu items and room rates in relation to market needs, adjusting prices up and down as appropriate. Using this approach we drew on the cost-plus and the going rate methods, shown in Figure 6.5, in order to arrive at an equitable price structure. This in fact constitutes our primary pricing decisions because it establishes the general menu charges and rack rates that we will normally offer to our customers.

Secondary pricing decisions

If our primary pricing decisions are carried out with care and sensitivity, and our products and services are of an acceptable quality, we should be in a position to attract reasonable numbers of customers. Nevertheless, however successful the approach proves to be we will usually experience low periods of demand resulting in spare capacity during certain days, weeks and months of the year. It is here where secondary pricing deci-

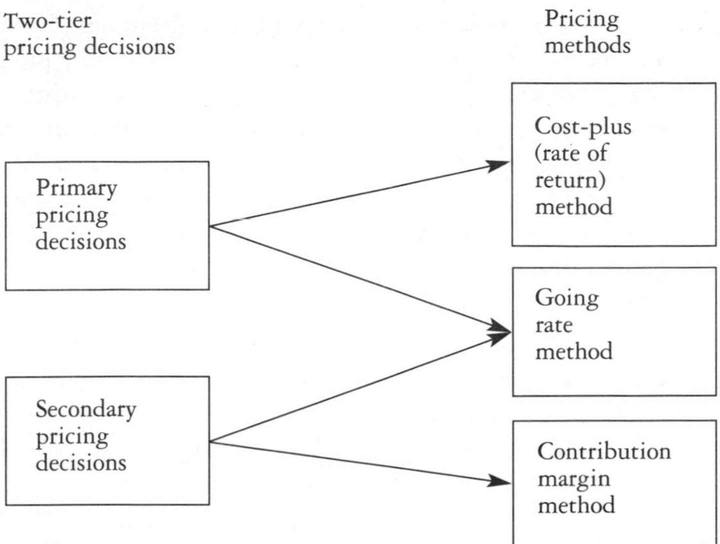

Figure 6.5 Developing an overall pricing policy

sions can be brought into good effect by combining the going rate and the contribution margin pricing methods, shown in Figure 6.5, to provide a flexible pricing tool to plug the gaps.

Because price is an important factor in generating revenue we can use the flexibility of contribution margin pricing to offer a variety of price-led incentives to attract additional custom. Examples of these are mid-week and weekend breaks, special prices for restaurant meals, parties and banquets on certain days, and happy-hour type refreshment sessions at pre-meal times. This should serve to increase the volume of restaurant customers and hotel guests, and support revenue and profit when business is slow or down on target.

Remember, providing the selling price is above variable cost each additional meal sold or room let will generate a contribution towards fixed costs and profit (explained in Chapter 5). As we explained at the outset, a feature of the hotel and catering industry is the relatively high proportion of fixed costs compared with industries such as manufacturing, and this can be used to advantage. If we refer to Figure 6.6 we can see that the higher the proportion of fixed costs the greater the range (or flexibility) of price discretion that is available.

So, prices can be set to attract additional business for meals and rooms, which in turn may cause a ripple effect by prompting customers to spend on drinks or perhaps gifts while they are visiting. However, a word of caution, contribution margin pricing is a powerful tool, but it should be used with thought and care. If used too liberally in short periods of low demand, or even in a recession, it can undermine the primary pricing policy because of market resistance to paying normal prices when conditions improve.

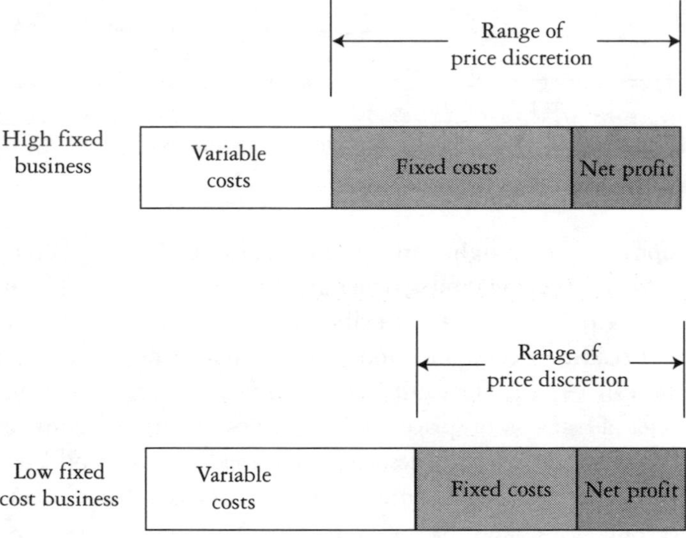

Figure 6.6 Effect of cost structure on pricing decisions

7 Profit improvement

How can we improve our profit? Should we aim to increase our sales revenue or reduce our costs, or what? These are the questions that managers constantly ask themselves in a bid to maintain or improve their profit position.

What influences profit?

Let us imagine for a moment that we are planning next year's budget and that we would like to improve on the current year's net profit by 10 per cent. In order to achieve this we could consider a number of basic options, such as:

- raising prices;
- increasing the volume of business;
- cutting costs;

or a combination of these options. However, if we increase price levels by 10 per cent will profit rise by 10 per cent? If we reduce costs by 10 per cent will profit increase by 10 per cent? We may have an intuitive feeling that certain factors increase or decrease profit by more or less than 10 per cent, but we are usually unable to be sure about the precise amount.

We may have in-built prejudices as to which factors have the greatest or least effect on profit, and therefore never take the time to determine if this is in fact the case. On the other hand we may have a reasonable impression of how certain factors affect profit in a particular hotel or restaurant business in which we have had previous experience and assume it is the same for all hotels and restaurants.

Key factors affecting net profit

If we are objectively to determine the influence that different 'critical' or 'key' factors have on net profit we first need to identify the factors and then determine the extent to which each one affects our profit. By doing this we will begin to build up a clearer picture of which factors have the greatest effect on the profitability of our business.

Most hotels and restaurants will have similar key factors regardless of the kind of service they provide. Figure 7.1 illustrates examples relating to a hotel. As we are able to quantify our operations in money terms we can group the key factors in terms of sales and cost items. The important point, however, is to determine the extent to which each factor affects net profit. To achieve this we can apply a simple technique know as 'profit sensitivity analysis'.

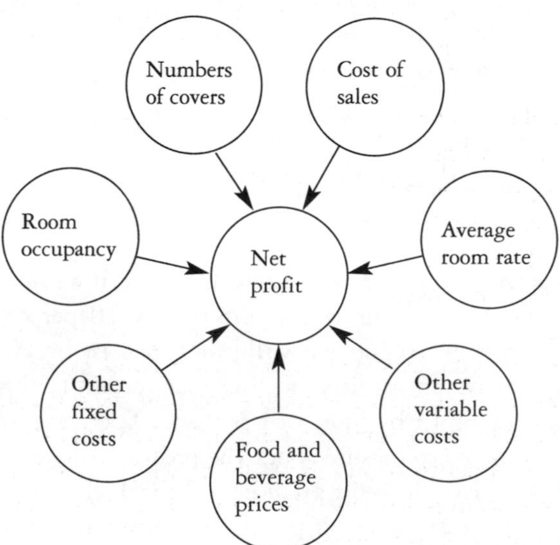

Figure 7.1 Examples of key factors that influence hotel net profit

Profit Sensitivity Analysis (PSA)

In order to carry out a profit sensitivity analysis we need to calculate the 'profit multipliers' of the business we are considering. The procedure is as follows:

1 Identify the key financial and operating factors of the business.
2 Assume a change in each key factor (say) 10 per cent.
3 Determine the resulting change in net profit caused by each key factor, holding other factors constant.
4 Compute the profit multipliers (PMs) by:

$$\text{PMs} = \frac{\%\text{ change in net profit}}{\%\text{ change in key factors}}$$

5 Rank the profit multipliers in order of magnitude and interpret the results.

An example

Let us see how the technique works by using the assumed results of the Riverside Restaurant for a typical week's trading, shown in Figure 7.2.

Referring to Figure 7.2 we can identify our restaurant's key factors as being:

- number of covers;
- average spend;
- food and beverage cost of sales;
- variable labour cost;
- fixed labour cost;
- other fixed costs.

If we now take each key factor in turn and assume a similar increase of 10 per cent, while holding other factors constant, we will be able to measure the separate effect each one has on net profit. In order to avoid repeatedly showing the detailed figures in our workings we will use the profit and loss statement in summary form, as follows:

Profit and loss statement (summary)

Sales revenue	£10,000
Less: total costs	£9,000
Net profit	£1,000

Number of covers (sales volume)

Sales volume + 10%

Sales revenue	£10,000	£11,000
Less: total costs	£9,000	£9,400
Net profit	£1,000	£1,600

NP + 60%

If we increase the number of covers by 10 per cent, assuming other factors remain constant, sales revenue will increase by £1,000, i.e. (500 × 0.10 × £20) to £11,000. Also with more customers, food and beverage cost, which is a variable cost, will increase by £300, i.e. (£3,000 × 0.10) as will variable labour cost by £100, i.e. (£1,000 × 0.10), thus increasing total cost by £400 to £9,400. The overall effect is to increase net profit by

Number of covers sold		500
Average spend		£20
Sales revenue–variable		£10,000
Less:		
Expenses		
Food and beverage–variable	£3,000	
Labour–variable	£1,000	
Labour–fixed	£2,000	
Other expenses–fixed	£3,000	£9,000
Net profit for week		£1,000

Note: Prior to applying PSA sales and cost items are required to be classified into their fixed and variable components, as explained in Chapter 5.

Figure 7.2 Riverside Restaurant. Profit and loss statement for one week

£600, i.e. (£1,000 × £400), to £1,600. Fixed costs will of course remain the same.

We can thus observe that a 10 per cent increase in the number of covers prompts a 60 per cent increase in net profit, calculated as follows:

$$\text{Increase in net profit} = \frac{£1{,}600 - £1{,}000}{£1{,}000} = \frac{£600}{£1{,}000} = 60 \text{ per cent}$$

We can now compute the profit multiplier for the number of covers as follows:

$$\text{PM} = \frac{\%\text{ change in net profit}}{\%\text{ change in key factor}} = \frac{60\%}{10\%} = +\,6.0$$

The profit multiplier of 6.0 indicates that for each 1 per cent *change* in the volume of sales the effect on our net profit is a six-fold increase. It therefore becomes clear that a small increase in the number of covers causes a disproportionate change in net profit. We can thus conclude that the Riverside Restaurant is sensitive to changes in the level of business.

Price level

	Prices + 10% →	
Sales revenue	£10,000	£11,000
Less: total costs	£9,000	£9,000
Net profit	£1,000	£2,000
	NP + 100%	

If we increase food and beverage prices by 10 per cent, assuming other factors remain constant, our net profit will rise by £1,000 to £2,000. As this does not entail an increase in the number of covers, variable costs, as well as fixed costs, will remain the same and the total benefit will drop to bottom-line profit. The percentage increase in net profit and the profit multiplier are calculated as follows:

$$\text{Increase in net profit} = \frac{£2{,}000 - £1{,}000}{£1{,}000}$$

$$= \frac{£1{,}000}{£1{,}000}$$

$$= 100\%$$

$$\text{PM} = \frac{100\%}{10\%}$$

$$= +\ 10.0$$

The price level profit multiplier indicates that for each 1 per cent change in food and beverage prices the effect on our net profit is a ten-fold increase. Therefore, a 10 per cent drop in prices would give a zero net profit, totally wiping out our weekly profit. It, therefore, becomes apparent that our restaurant's net profit is even more sensitive to changes in price levels than sales volume (number of covers).

Having understood the principles involved in performing a profit sensitivity analysis on our first two key factors, the remaining four factors are completed in a similar manner, the results of which are given below:

Food and beverage costs

		F & B Costs + 10%
Sales revenue	£10,000	£10,000
Less: total costs	£9,000	£9,300
Net profit	£1,000	£700
		NP–

Only food and beverage costs increase by 10 per cent, other factors remain constant (no other revenue or cost changes) resulting in the following position:

$$\text{Decrease in net profit} = \frac{£700 - £1{,}000}{£1{,}000}$$

$$= \frac{-\ £300}{£1{,}000}$$

$$= -\ 30\%$$

$$PM = \frac{-\ 30\%}{10\%}$$

$$= -\ 3.0$$

Hence, for each 1 per cent increase in food and beverage costs the effect on net profit is three times greater.

Labour cost–variable

		Var. labour + 10%
Sales revenue	£10,000	£10,000
Less: total cost	£9,000	£9,100
Net profit	£1,000	£900
	NP – 10%	

Again, in the case where only variable labour cost increases the computations are as follows:

$$\text{Decrease in net profit} = \frac{£900 - £1{,}000}{£1{,}000}$$

$$= \frac{-\ 100}{£1{,}000}$$

$$= -\ 10\%$$

$$PM = \frac{-\ 10\%}{10\%}$$

$$= -\ 1.0$$

The change in net profit is – 10 per cent and, therefore, the PM = – 1.0.

Labour cost–fixed

		Fixed labour + 10%
Sales revenue	£10,000	£10,000
Less: total cost	£9,000	£9,200
Net profit	£1,000	£800
	NP – 20%	

The change in net profit is – 20 per cent and therefore, the PM = – 2.0.

Other costs–fixed

	Other fixed + 10%	
Sales revenue	£10,000	£10,000
Less: total costs	£9,000	£9,300
Net profit	£1,000	£700
	NP – 30%	

The change in net profit is – 30 per cent and thus, the PM = – 3.0

Figure 7.3 shows a summary of our profit sensitivity analysis. Notice the plus and minus signs; the revenue PMs are positive and the cost PMs are negative because we assumed an increase in key factors. If we had assumed a decrease of 10 per cent in the key factors the revenue PMs would show as negative and the cost PMs would show as positive. Hence, as the PM values remain the same we can ignore the arithmetical signs and focus our attention on the impact on profit of a *change* (increase or decrease) in key factors. Thus, as a 10 per cent change in the sales volume of our Riverside Restaurant will have a six-fold effect on net profit the PM will simply be 6.0.

PMs based on 10 per cent increase in key factors

Key factor	Current profit £	New profit £	Profit change %	PMs
Number of covers	1,000	1,600	+60	+6.0
Price level	1,000	2,000	+100	+10.0
F&B costs—variable	1,000	700	– 30	– 3.0
Labour cost—variable	1,000	9000	– 10	– 1.0
Labour cost—fixed	1,000	800	– 20	– 2.0
Other costs—fixed	1,000	700	– 30	– 3.0

Note: Do not calculate too many PMs, i.e. more than five or six, or the effect of PSA will be lost

Figure 7.3 Riverside Restaurant. Profit Sensitivity Analysis summary

Note also that we have used 10 per cent in our illustration. This is only for convenience and ease of calculation. Whatever level of percentage change is used the profit multipliers will remain the same for a particular business.

Understanding PSA results

Now that we have determined how net profit is affected by changes in the Riverside Restaurant's key factors we can view the overall profit multiplier profile, presented in Figure 7.4 and interpret our findings. The object of this is to identify the business orientation and accounting and control strategy that should be adopted by our restaurant in order to improve its profitability.

Business orientation

From Figure 7.4 we can see that the revenue-based PMs, above the broken line, have the highest values and therefore, the greatest impact on the net profit. In contrast the cost-based PM values are all lower and thus have less influence on the profit. This indicates that our restaurant is a market oriented establishment and that sales generation is crucial.

PMs ranked in order of magnitude

Key factor	*PMs*
Price level	10.0
Number of covers	6.0
F & B costs–variable	3.0
Other–fixed	3.0
Labour–fixed	2.0
Labour–variable	1.0

Figure 7.4 Riverside Restaurant. Profit Multiplier profile

Accounting strategy

As the revenue side of the restaurant is more important we are required to take a 'revenue accounting' approach to business. This means that our records should facilitate the recording and analysis of revenue activities in considerable detail in order to highlight areas of potential improvement. Management reports should emphasize items such as average spend, sales volume, sales mix, gross margins and contribution margins. In the case of a hotel this should also include room occupancy, average room rate and perhaps percentage repeat business.

Control strategy

Because the revenue side of the restaurant has a greater impact on profitability this acts as a guide to the amount of time and effort we should allocate to control activities. In the case of our restaurant the PM profile indicates that we should expend a greater proportion of our time and effort controlling revenue-associated areas than controlling costs.

While the market oriented nature of the restaurant requires us to concentrate our time on revenue related areas this does not suggest that cost control should be neglected. Indeed, controlling costs is an essential function in most businesses. The point to remember is that our major efforts should normally be directed towards the area that has the greatest influence on profit, which in the Riverside Restaurant's case is revenue generation and control.

Market and cost oriented businesses

Our example above has centred around a restaurant business so let us now consider the profit multiplier profiles of two other hospitality businesses, namely a luxury hotel and an airline catering contractor. The assumed PM profiles of the two businesses are presented in Figure 7.5.

Luxury hotel		*Airline catering contractor*	
(Market oriented business)		(Cost oriented business)	
Key factor	*PM*	*Key factor*	*PM*
Price level	12.0*	Price level	5.0
Sales volume	9.0*	Cost of sales	3.0*
Operating costs – fixed	6.0	Sales volume	2.5
Dept labour – fixed	4.0	Payroll – variable	2.0*
Dept labour – variable	3.5†	Overheads – fixed	0.5
F & B costs – variable	2.0†	Overheads – variable	0.5†
*Prime areas for control			
†Secondary areas for control			

Figure 7.5 Market and cost oriented profit multiplier profiles

Luxury hotel–a market oriented example

Referring to Figure 7.5 we can see that the hotel is clearly a market oriented establishment and indeed heavily reliant upon, and sensitive to, revenue-based key factors. The highest PM values are price level and sales volume at 12.0 and 9.0 respectively, higher than their Riverside Restaurant counterparts which we recall are 10.0 and 6.0 respectively. The difference will mainly be due to the rooms sales element which generates high profit margins. Thus, the emphasis of the hotel's management team should be on revenue generation and control and, to a lesser degree, the control of department variable labour and food and beverage costs. Fixed operating costs and department labour costs cannot usually be influenced in the short term.

Airline catering contractor–a cost oriented example

In contrast to the luxury hotel, or Riverside Restaurant for that matter, the airline catering contractor's PM profile provides us with an excellent example of a cost-oriented business. The price level will usually be fixed annually with the airlines and the sales volume will normally be determined by the airline's need. Thus, both the revenue-based PMs are outside the control of the catering contractor. Therefore, the most appropriate control strategy to maintain profitability is to concentrate on cost of sales, variable payroll and to a lesser extent variable overhead. Clearly, additional airline business will improve the contractor's profit, but cultivating contracts is normally a lengthy process.

PSA: a framework for profit improvement

Profit improvement is often an important aim for most commercially related businesses, but it is rarely an easy objective to achieve. However, as we have tried to show, PSA provides us with a basic framework for developing a profit improvement programme. In summary PSA can assist us in the following ways:

1 *Measuring the relative impact of key factors on net profit.* This provides us with an insight into profitability.
2 *Identifying business orientation.* Is our business cost or market oriented?
3 *Determining the accounting emphasis.* Should we develop an appropriate revenue accounting approach or rely on the more traditional cost accounting procedures and systems?
4 *Determining a control strategy.* How should we allocate our time? Should we expend more effort on controlling revenue or costs?
5 *Identifying the most fruitful areas for profit improvement.* Will we benefit more by reducing costs, increasing sales volume or raising prices?
6 *Budgeting and profit planning.* Which areas are important in terms of us achieving accurate predictions?

A criticism of PSA

An important criticism levelled at PSA is that the impact on net profit prompted by a percentage change in a key factor is determined while all other factors are held constant. It is reasonably argued that, for instance, if we raise prices then demand will probably fall, and thus the real effect should be seen in the context of the total impact caused by all the factors. This is fair comment, but in order for us to make an informed judgement on the overall impact caused by the combination effect of several key factor changes we must first assess the magnitude of each factor. By doing this we will usually be in a better position both to determine the factor that should be changed at the outset and to evaluate its likely effect on other key areas. We have, in fact, borrowed the scientist's tried and tested technique of isolating and measuring the individual effect of different elements in a controlled experiment.

8 Budgets and forecasting

Financial planning encompasses a wide range of topics, from credit control to investment decisions. However, they all require accurate predictions of the level of business to be achieved in the future, whether expressed in terms of cash received, payments to be made or the necessity for large-scale loans to fund a new acquisition. The process for predicting these levels of business is known as *forecasting*.

We will consider several different types of forecast, dependent on the time-scale involved and on the specific information required. A *budget* is a formalized forecast, for a specific time period (usually one year), whereas the usual industry definition of a forecast is of a less-detailed prediction, for a time-span of anything from a day to ten years.

Budgets

Budgets are formal forecasts of the level of business or trading to be achieved. They are usually very detailed, and are generally completed for the next full financial year, by month.

Why prepare budgets?

A budget is a *strategic plan* which guides our steps for the year. It consists not only of financial information, but also of the actions required of us in order to achieve these monetary targets. A budget does not consist only of numbers, but also of various reports and charts. For instance, a finished budget will include a marketing plan and a staff organization chart, neither of which reports may include any numbers at all (although these will appear later on separate pages).

The finalized budget is used as a measure of performance – we can compare how well we are performing with how well we expect to perform. Companies are increasingly making their managers more responsible for the financial results of their areas, and often pay increases and promotion will depend on this. With these types of incentives, managers need as much information as possible to be able to take decisions on a daily basis, and to be able to communicate effectively with their staff.

At a higher level, companies must budget accurately in order to be able to maintain the confidence of their shareholders, to borrow money from financial institutions and to plan their overall company strategies for the future.

Types of budget

There are different sections of a *master budget* which, when combined, will form a full financial plan for the forthcoming year. These are:

- *Operating budget*. A plan for the revenue and expenditure to be achieved during the period. This forms the largest section of the master budget, and involves decision making by all members of the hotel or restaurant's management team. The format of the operations budget closely resembles a profit and loss statement.
- *Cash budget*. A plan of the movement of cash in and out of the business. This is derived from the information in the operations budget, and is usually completed by the unit financial managers.

- *Capital budget*. A plan for the expenditure required in terms of large equipment and refurbishment projects needed to achieve the levels of revenue detailed in the operations budget.

Together the cash and capital budgets would form a budgeted balance sheet.

The budgeting process

The budget team

We can compare the budget team to a football team. There is a manager, a coach, a team of players with a captain, a rule book and even a pitch. There is also a governing body who make the final decisions as to results, with a referee to adjudicate at a lower level.

- *The manager*. The manager of the budget is usually the general manager of the operation, whether it is a hotel, a resort complex or a catering unit. This person is ultimately responsible for the content of the budget, and for actually achieving the results predicted.
- *The coach*. The financial controller of the operation will act as the coach. This person needs to be fully conversant with all the rules required of the 'game' and to act as a mediator between the players and the manager.
- *The captain and players*. There may well be several captains with several teams of players within the operation. In a large hotel, for instance, there will be a separate group for each discipline (rooms area, food and beverage, administration, etc.) all with different sections of the budget to complete, but all dependent on each other. Smaller units may only have one budget team, and the manager may also act in a captain's capacity. The hotel or restaurant is, of course, *the pitch*.
- *The rule book*. This is the budget manual, which specifies which information is to be detailed in the budget, and also may give other criteria to be used (see below). Where the operation is part of a large organization, this will usually be

prepared by a head office, which actually decides the rules of the game.

- *The governing body*. The head office, where it exists, forms the governing body. In all cases, the operation (whether it be a single restaurant or a multinational hotel corporation) will be ultimately responsible to its shareholders or owners, who will decide what return on investment they require from the business. This will result in the formation of many of the rules or criteria necessary. There may well be a *referee* in the guise of a regional controller or operations manager.

Preliminary processes

Before the commencement of the budgeting process, and before many of the departmental managers become involved, we need to obtain certain information. This may well be supplied by a head office, which will make preliminary decisions as to future events.

Market trends

This is probably the most important aspect of the budgeting process. Accurate and detailed predictions of the demand for the product are essential if an effective and achievable budget is to be prepared. We should determine:

- competition for the product (other hotels, a new restaurant locally);
- the prices that can be charged for the type of clientele to be attracted;
- new products that we can offer (in-room technology, leisure facilities);
- inflation factors;
- foreign exchange rates (influence the level of overseas tourist activity);
- the weather (influences local trade);
- international political activity;
- fashion (what is popular today may not be popular tomorrow);

- how much we can afford in terms of marketing and advertising in order to maintain or increase our level of trade;
- how much we can afford in terms of new systems and what options and benefits these offer.

All this information forms the major part of the *sales and marketing plan* (see page 122).

Expense trends

Inflation factors also have a major influence on the level of expenditure we are permitted. This information will include predictions on the level of price rises of fresh foods, beverages, utilities and so on, as well as the projected increase in pay levels allowed.

Prior results

In order to predict the level of business in the future, accurate records of prior achievement are essential. This will include past departmental profit and loss reports, statistics on types of rooms and covers sold, sources of business and rates achieved.

Limiting factors

We cannot always budget for what we want. There are various limitations on the level of business we can achieve. Some of these are:

- *Capacity*. It is difficult to sell 110 rooms if you have a country hotel with only 100 bedrooms, banqueting suites will have a maximum number of guests allowed (may be determined by fire regulations as well as space).
- *Labour*. The availability and affordability of certain categories of staff may determine what type of operation you have.
- *Equipment*. The type of equipment available may restrict the service provided.
- *Management*. Do you have the right quality of manager?

- *Capital*. The cost of replacing or upgrading furniture, fixtures and equipment (particularly technological equipment which can have a short life-span) can be very high and may not be justifiable.
- *Systems*. Do you have the right systems to support what you want to do ?

Putting the budget together

This section assumes that plenty of past information is available. If little prior data exists, then please refer to the section on 'Zero-based budgeting' (page 131). This applies wherever significant changes have taken place in the type of operation being budgeted for (e.g. changes in concept, new units, etc).

Referring to Figure 8.1 we will now follow through the 'planning route' using assumed figures for the Country House Hotel. Note that all figures used in the example are stated net of Value Added Tax (VAT).

Head office

Earlier in our discussion we mentioned the information that may be supplied to the hotel and restaurant by the head office (if it exists), or determined locally if the operation is independent. Examples of this include return on investment decisions, market trend information and prior results.

Sales and marketing plan

In a hotel, this will be prepared by a sales and marketing manager or possibly (in a smaller unit) by someone at head office level. This is the master plan for *how* we will achieve *what* we want to achieve. From the information available and decisions already taken (see 'Market trends' on page 120), the sales manager and general manager will decide the average room rate and room occupancy that should be budgeted. In the case of a restaurant company, they will decide the total customers and average spend achievable.

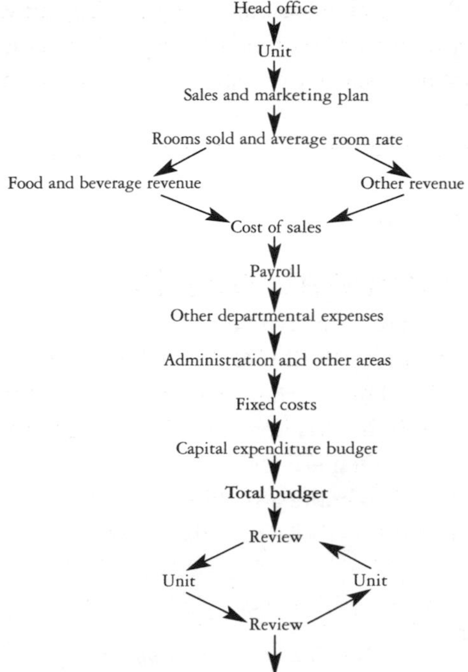

Figure 8.1 Budgets – planning route

Once the targets have been agreed, then decisions are made as to the resources and actions required to achieve them, in terms of advertising, additional sales executives, public relations and so on.

Rooms revenue, occupancy and average room rate

The rooms revenue is calculated from the budgeted rooms sold (occupancy) and budget average room rate (ARR). Most hotels spend a great deal of time and effort in deciding these items, and will build up to a total from the market *segmentation analysis* of the previous year.

Segmentation splits the total of rooms sold by day of the week and by type of business. A simple segment would be tours, conferences, full-rate, split by weekend and weekday – a total of six categories. Some large hotels have up to 14 types of business, and will calculate *each day* separately (98 categories per week). If you then divide these further into the different types of room available (singles, doubles, executive rooms, suites, etc.) then it becomes obvious why so many hotels now use complex computer spreadsheet or yield management models to help them plan their budgets!

An example of budgeting

The Country House Hotel has 30 bedrooms and a restaurant. During the week it relies heavily on conference trade (a package rate including all meals) and tourists at the weekend.

In past years, the level of trade has been determined, and the decision made not to increase occupancy further (or the number of covers), but to implement increased prices in order to cover increased costs (and to make a little more profit).

Information relating to the hotel is as follows:

Average rooms sold per night for June

	Mon-Thurs	*Fri-Sun*
Tours	5	22
Conferences	15	0
Full rate	2	4

If June has four weeks then there are four each Monday to Thursday (total 16 nights) and four each Friday to Sunday (total 12 nights).

Total rooms sold

	Mon-Thurs	*Fri-Sun*	*Total*
Tours	80	264	344
Conferences	240	0	240
Full rate	32	48	80
Total	352	312	664

The total rooms *available* is (28 nights × 30 rooms) = 840, so the occupancy achieved will be 79.1 per cent.

For the average spend, you need to decide the new ARR achievable for each segment (net of VAT) per night, and multiply by the number of rooms. It should be noted that 'rooms' revenue here relates only to that portion of an inclusive rate that relates to accommodation. It does not include the amount allocated to breakfast, for instance. Here, last year's achieved ARR has been increased by 10 per cent, and rounded.

	Rooms	*ARR*	*Revenue*
		£	£
Tours	344	41.25	14,190
Conferences	240	45.65	10,956
Full rate	80	68.75	5,500
Total	664		30,646

The overall ARR will be £46.15.

From the rooms sold you can determine the number of beds to be occupied (sleepers). If this hotel sells all its tour and full rate rooms to two people, and all its conference rooms to one person, then the sleepers are:

	Rooms	*Per room*	*Sleepers*
Tours	344	2	688
Conferences	240	1	240
Full rate	80	2	160
Total	664		1,088

We now have a rooms revenue budget for June, and just need to repeat the process 11 or 12 more times for the rest of the year! Once the occupancy and sleepers have been agreed, then the other revenue can be decided.

Food and beverage

Restaurant: a combination of in-house guests and others.

Breakfast: how many sleepers have breakfast? For this example we estimate that they all do, giving a total of 1,088 breakfasts.

Lunch and dinner: estimate for each different segment the percentage of guests who eat in the restaurant

Lunch

	Sleepers	Percentage eating	Covers
Tours	688	20	138
Conferences	240	100	240
Full rate	160	5	8
Total			386

Dinner

	Sleepers	Percentage eating	Covers
Tours	688	80	550
Conferences	240	100	240
Full rate	160	30	48
Total			838

Add on customers from outside – here an average of 10 per day, dinner only (equals an extra 280 dinner covers for June). The food and beverage revenue is calculated in the same way as the rooms revenue – that is, covers times average spend. The average spend is usually last year plus a percentage increase according to the estimated menu price increases.

	Breakfast	Lunch	Dinner	Total
Covers	1,088	386	1,118	2,592
	£	£	£	£
Food spend	8.15	10.95	15.00	11.52
Beverage spend	0	1.90	5.95	2.85
Total				14.37
	£	£	£	£
Food revenue	8,867	4,227	16,770	29,864
Beverage revenue	0	733	6,652	7,385
Total	8,867	4,960	23,422	37,249

The 'total' spends are an average of all meal times i.e. the total revenue divided by the total covers. In the above example the overall beverage spend is £2.85, which includes breakfast covers. Some companies perceive it as more technically correct to include only lunch and dinner covers in the average beverage spend calculation which would give £4.91. Providing that they are always consistent, either approach may be used.

Where there are no rooms, then all trade is 'outside' and the budget is based on knowledge of these numbers from prior years. In our example there are no other food and beverage outlets. If the hotel had a banqueting suite, then the budget covers are derived from information on past year figures plus advance bookings in the banqueting diary. Bar figures are based on last year plus an increase, although where many residents use the bar, you should estimate an average spend per sleeper. Room service is also based on a spend per sleeper, unless they also service meeting rooms in which case a separate set of figures is required.

Other revenue

Other revenue is also derived from sleeper counts and last year's spend plus an increase, for example:

Telephone: average spend last year £1.16, plus 8 per cent

Sleepers	*Spend*	*Revenue*
1,088	£1.25	£1,360

Total revenue

We have now worked out the total revenue budget:

			£
Rooms			30,646
F & B	Food	29,864	
	Beverage	7,385	37,249
Telephone			1,360
Total			69,255

There are very many more criteria for calculating the revenue for a particular operation. For instance:

- Particular weeks of the year may be busier than others (e.g. local race meetings).
- The hotel may offer a day-rate-only conference package.
- Special promotions may be made for certain days of the week (e.g. 'happy hour' on Monday).
- Average spends in the restaurant may be higher on Saturdays.

Cost of sales

The cost of sales percentages are normally based on those achieved in prior years. To find the cost of sales:

	Sales	*Cost*	*Sales*
	£	%	£
Food	29,864	38.0	11,348
Beverage	7,385	32.0	2,363
Telephone	1,360	40.0	544

Payroll

Payroll is usually calculated by using the zero-base concept (see p. 131) as this is one of the highest (and often most contentious) cost areas. Rarely do hotels and restaurants just take a prior year figure and add an increase for pay rises, but more often will prepare a full list of all job categories – a *headcount budget*. When the 'heads' are multiplied by the pay rate, and benefits added, then the payroll budget results. (Benefits include National Insurance, sick pay, staff travel, meals on duty, etc.)

In large hotels, the staffing of the housekeeping area (for instance) may be *directly* related to the number of beds, and the room attendants budgeted in terms of average cost per room (based on cost of time to clean one bedroom). This works only where there are sufficient staff with a fairly high turnover to be able to adjust the numbers employed on a weekly basis. Budgeting payroll by occupancy may also be possible with a very flexible work-force, who are to work only when required. For example:

Room attendants last year + 8% pay rise
Four staff × pay rate £162 (£150 + 8%) = £648/week
Add 10% benefits = £2,851 for June.

Other departmental costs

Costs are divided into fixed and variable (see Chapter 5) and are budgeted as such:

- *Variable costs* relate to volume, or occasionally as a percentage of sales (e.g. commissions), for example:

  Linen last year plus 10% cost increase
  Sleepers 1,088 × £1.63 (£1.48 + 10%) = £1,773 for June
  Covers 2,592 × £0.62 (£0.56 + 10%) = £1,607

- *Fixed costs* are calculated as last year plus a percentage increase, unless you specifically know otherwise.

Departmental profit statement

After all costs have been calculated, then the departmental profit report can be assembled, for example:

Telephone	£
Revenue	1,360
Cost of sales	(544)
Gross profit	816
Payroll	(740)
Other costs	(71)
Departmental profit	5

Remember, it is an *essential service* department, although a profit is a bonus!

Administration

At the same time as the operating departments are preparing their budgets, managers in the administration areas should determine their payroll and other costs. Administration includes general management, repairs and maintenance, sales and marketing and accounting – all those departments that *service* the entire hotel and cannot be allocated to a specific profit centre.

Costs are based on prior year figures, plus an increase for inflation.

Fixed costs

Generally the fixed costs cannot be controlled by the hotel, but are predetermined either by the company or outside agencies. For instance:

- *Rates*: the Uniform Business Rate is set by the local authority.
- *Interest*: may be a fixed rate, but may also be determined by the bank who lent the money.
- *Depreciation*: depreciation for new capital expenditure may be controllable (do we or do we not undertake this project?) but that for prior years must be budgeted for.

Final budget and review process

Once all the figures have been gathered, we must assemble the total budget package. This usually takes the form of a file containing all the departmental statements and statistics, plus all relevant supporting documentation (e.g. sales and marketing plan, headcount chart).

The 'final' budget is presented to head office (or owners, if they have not been involved in the earlier processes). Frequently, they will require changes in revenue and costs, which means that someone (often the controller) must amend all the necessary numbers to produce a new profit figure. This review-amend-review process can happen several times before the budget is finally approved.

(Most managers 'hold something up their sleeve', knowing that their first numbers won't be acceptable – it is all part of the 'game'.)

What happens if we don't have any past information?

There may well be occasions when past data either does not exist or is unusable:

- for a brand new unit (hotel, restaurant, etc);
- a refurbished outlet with a new concept (e.g. café, where previously there was a steak bar);
- a new product (e.g. serving meals in a bar);
- if the hotel has been sold and the previous owners have taken all the documents with them.

In any of these cases, we need to *zero base* our budget.

Zero basing requires starting from scratch, with as much (or as little) information as possible. There is always *some* information which can be used, even if this is only based on the previous experience of the manager. A lot of decisions will, of necessity, be based on guesswork.

For instance

Mall Café – a new cafe in a shopping precinct, seating 40 persons. The shopping precinct closes at 6 p.m. daily.

A sales and marketing plan *should* have been drawn up as part of the initial planning of the project (and would be required by any bank from which you were trying to borrow money). This will have included the use of market research to find out from passers-by whether or not they would use such a facility, and the type of opposition available (other cafés, pubs, fast food outlets).

Revenue

Potential customers are:

Morning	100	mainly coffees, some pastries
Lunch	60	limited by number of seats
Afternoon	80	mainly teas, half will have scones etc.

So the total customers will be *240*.

Average spends can be calculated from the food consumed:

	Spend	*Revenue*
Morning – coffee	100 × £1.00	£100
pastries	20 × £1.15	£ 23
Lunch	60 × £4.10	£246
Afternoon – teas	80 × £0.75	£ 60
scones	40 × £1.80	£ 72
Total daily revenue (ex VAT)		£501

The daily average spend (£501 divided by 240 covers) is £2.09.

Cost of sales

This is based on the actual cost of the ingredients:

	Cost	Cost of sales
Morning – coffee	100 × £0.30	£ 30
pastries	20 × £0.75	£15
Lunch	60 × £2.60	£156
Afternoon – teas	80 × £0.25	£ 20
scones	40 × £0.70	£ 28
Total daily costs		£249
Total daily gross profit		£252 or 50 per cent

Payroll

Payroll must be calculated based on the number of staff required, at a particular pay rate, for example:

One full time manager at	= £225/week
One full time general assistant	= £140/week
Two part time assistants working	
15 hours each at £3.50/hour	= each £52.50/week
Total £470 plus 10% benefits	= £517 per week

Other costs

To calculate these, you need to know exactly what items you will need to run the business, for example:

> Paper napkins – 240 customers per day using one each, plus wastage = approximately 250/day = 1 packet. How much is a packet of napkins?

For less tangible items such as electricity you may need to rely on prior knowledge, although it is possible to work out the consumption of units, multiply by the price and add standing charges in order to find the total cost.

Fixed costs should be known, as with a normal budget.

Forecasting

A forecast is a type of budget, but is usually completed on a short-term basis and is generally much less detailed. A budget is usually completed up to a year ahead, and many factors may change which require a more up-to-date prediction of the level of business.

We need to forecast:

- *Daily*. 'Do we have space that we need to fill tonight?' 'Can I send a waiter home?'
- *Weekly*. 'Do I need to sell rooms for next week?' 'Do we need an extra room attendant?'
- *Monthly*. 'If next month is quiet we can use up some of those outstanding staff holidays.'
- *Seasonally*. 'There's a projection of a tourist boom. I need to make sure my rates are competitive but not too cheap.' 'Will I need to open the bar all day to cater for these extra tourists?'

What do we forecast?

We forecast:

- rooms sold and average rate;
- food and beverage covers and spends;
- other revenue;
- cost of sales;
- payroll;
- expenses;

leading to a projected profit and loss statement.

Why do we forecast?

We forecast to enable *managers* to plan more effectively.

- *Rooms sold*: selling strategy.
- Maximize occupancy and rate; staffing requirements.
- *Covers*: reservation strategy; staffing requirements; open/closure policy.
- *Cost of sales*: ordering of food and beverage.
- *Payroll*: staffing requirements in all areas; overtime, bank holidays, holidays.
- *Expenses*: ordering, storage, issues, usage; price controls.

We also forecast to enable *financial management* to control more effectively:

- Revenue: cash flow, debtors, foreign exchange.
- Expenditure: cash flow, creditors, purchasing.

What do we do next?

There is little point in budgeting and forecasting if the numbers are not used by managers on a daily and periodic basis. We need to compare the number we budgeted with those that *actually* occurred, analyse the differences and find out:

- What we do wrong, and what we can do to make it better.
- What we did right – let's try to do it again.

Forcasting allows us to identify short-term problems, and hopefully to take some actions as a result in order to minimize our risks.

How do we make this budgeting easier?

By using a computer spreadsheet!

Many companies design spreadsheets for their managers in order to help them prepare their budgets and forecasts. Simple spreadsheets can be designed by most users, to make the calculations easier to handle (and to save time). This is explained and illustrated in Chapter 10.

Use of 'what if?' functions (what would happen to my profits if we increased our rooms sold by five per night?) can answer many of the queries posed *accurately* and *quickly*, and allow managers time to spend on making decisions, rather than on calculating the numbers.

9 Budgets for planning and control

In the previous chapter we explained the process involved in forecasting revenue and expenses and preparing an annual budget. When the budget has been prepared we need to be able to gain some idea of what to expect if we don't achieve our anticipated level of business. We also want to be in a position to compare actual results with budget so we can monitor our progress and take appropriate action for the future. In this chapter we will consider further how budgets can help us in profit planning and how budgets can assist us in controlling our operations.

Budgets for planning

What happens if we fail to achieve our budget target? For instance we may have anticipated hotel room occupancy to be 75 per cent in the coming year and in the event only achieve 60 per cent. How would a 15 per cent shortfall in occupancy affect our projected annual profit? If we had some insight into the likely consequences we could make preliminary plans to remedy the situation should it arise.

Flexible budgets

An effective way to determine the likely position if we under- or over-achieve projected results is to prepare a 'flexible' budget prior to the start of the budget period. A flexible budget is simply a budget that can be adjusted or 'flexed' to take account of different levels of sales volume. It does, however, involve analysing our annual budgeted revenues and costs into their fixed and variable components, as explained in Chapter 5. Once this is done we can adjust revenues and costs in line with various levels of sales volume and thereby determine how profit is affected.

Let us consider an example using the assumed figures of the Anchor Hotel, a 50-room establishment that is open all the year round. The budget committee have prepared the annual projections for the coming year and analysed the expenses into their fixed and variable categories, as shown in Figure 9.1.

The next step is to assemble the annual projections into budget format, illustrated in Figure 9.2. We can see from Figure 9.2 that if our actual results exactly match the budget the hotel will generate £55,000 net profit. Since this is highly unlikely, especially in terms of the volume of business, we need to assess the effect on costs and profit if variations do occur.

Preparing a flexible budget

In order to estimate how costs and profits will respond to a sales shortfall or overshoot we need to extend our budgeted profit and loss statement into a flexible budget. Remember, the reason for preparing a flexible budget is to enable us to assess our position if the actual level of business differs from the annual budget.

Let us consider the situation where our general level of business varies by 10 per cent, i.e. where both occupancy and restaurant business varies. Figure 9.3 shows the results.

Number of rooms	50
Average room rate	£40
Room occupancy	70%
Food revenue	£200,000
Beverage revenue	£100,000

Rooms payroll and other expenses:
Variable –10% of rooms revenue
Fixed – £86,870

Food and beverage expenses:
Food cost – 40% of food sales
Beverage cost – 30% of beverage sales
Payroll and other expenses:
Variable – 15% of F & B sales
Fixed – £60,000

Undistributed operating expenses (fixed) and fixed charges – £403,030

Figure 9.1 The Anchor Hotel. Annual budget projections (for next year)

The workings for our flexible budget in Figure 9.3 are given below. *Note*: calculations are for the *10 per cent less* than budget situation.

Rooms department:
Room sales = £511,000 × 0.9 = £459,900
The same result is achieved if we reduce occupancy by the shortfall:
New occupancy = 0.7 × 0.9 = 0.63
Thus, 50 × 365 × 0.63 × £40 = £459,900

Rooms payroll and other expenses (variable)
= £459,900 × 0.1 = £45,990

Rooms payroll and other expenses (fixed)
This amount remains the same at £86,870

	£	
Room sales	511,000	(50 × 365 × 0.7 × £40)
Payroll and other expenses		
Variable (10%)	51,100	(£511,000 × 0.10)
Fixed	86,870	
Total	137,970	
Department profit	373,030	(£511,000–£137,970)
Restaurant sales		
Food	200,000	
Beverage	100,000	
Total	300,000	
Food cost (40%)	80,000	(£200,000 × 0.40)
Beverage cost (30%)	30,000	(£100,000 × 0.30)
Total	110,000	
Gross profit	190,000	(£300,000 – £110,000)
Payroll and other expenses		
Variable (15%)	45,000	(£300,000 × 0.15)
Fixed	60,000	
Total	105,000	
Department profit	85,000	
Total department profit	458,030	(£373,030 + £85,000)
Undistributed operating expenses and fixed charges	403,030	
Net profit before tax	£55,000	

Figure 9.2 The Anchor Hotel
Budgeted profit and loss statement for next year

Restaurant department:

Food sales = £200,000 × 0.9 = £180,000
Beverage sales = £100,000 × 0.9 = £ 90,000
Food cost = £180,000 × 0.4 = £ 72,000
Beverage cost = £ 90,000 × 0.3 = £ 27,000
Restaurant payroll and other expenses (variable)

	10% less	Budget	10% more
	£	£	£
Room sales	459,900	511,000	562,100
Payroll and other expenses			
Variable (10%)	45,990	51,100	56,210
Fixed	86,870	86,870	86,870
Total	132,860	137,970	143,080
Department profit	327,040	373,030	419,020
Restaurant sales			
Food	180,000	200,000	220,000
Beverage	90,000	100,000	110,000
Total	270,000	300,000	330,000
Food cost (40%)	72,000	80,000	88,000
Beverage cost (30%)	27,000	30,000	33,000
Total	99,000	110,000	121,000
Gross profit	171,000	190,000	209,000
Payroll and other expenses			
Variable (15%)	40,500	45,000	49,500
Fixed	60,000	60,000	60,000
Total	100,500	105,000	109,500
Department profit	70,500	85,000	99,500
Total department profit	397,540	458,030	518,520
Undistributed operating expenses and fixed charges	403,030	403,030	403,030
Net profit/(loss)	(5,490)	55,000	115,490

Figure 9.3 The Anchor Hotel
Flexible budget for next year

= £270,000 × 0.5 = £40,500
Restaurant payroll and other expenses (fixed)
This amount remains the same at £60,000

Our flexible budget shows that if we exceed budget by 10 per cent, net profit will rise dramatically from £55,000 to £115,490, which is an increase of 110 per cent. However, if we experience a shortfall of 10 per cent our net profit will be wiped out and turned into a loss of £5,490. So in the case of the Anchor Hotel a 10 per cent change in demand results in a 110 per cent change in net profit, i.e. a small change in demand causes a large change in profit. Clearly, the hotel is a market oriented business that relies heavily on the level of sales volume to maintain its profits.

Knowing in advance what sales, costs and profit are likely to be if we fail to achieve budget is extremely helpful. It gives us the opportunity to consider alternative courses of action ahead of time, rather than simply reacting hastily to a crisis. We may regard it as prudent to make preliminary investigations into alternative sources of revenue or perhaps arrange our staffing so as to cause minimal disruption to the level of service if we need to cut costs. These and many other possibilities can be contemplated as a result of using a flexible budget for planning purposes.

Budgets for control

We have seen how the flexible budget can help us in planning, so what of control? At the end of the budget period we will usually find that our actual results differ from budget. We need to identify the sources of these differences, called 'variances', so that we can determine the causes and take appropriate action for the future. As we will see, the flexible budget can aid us with this task.

Let us consider the assumed summary results of the Acorn Restaurant which are given in Figure 9.4.

	Budget		Actual	
Number of covers	20,000		25,000	
	£	%	£	%
Sales revenue	240,000	100	287,500	100
Less: food cost	84,000	35	117,000	40.7
Gross profit	156,000	65	170,500	59.3

Figure 9.4 The Acorn Restaurant
Summary results

We can see that budgeted sales have risen giving a gross profit increase of £14,500, i.e. £170,500 – £156,000, but that gross profit percentage has fallen by 5.7 per cent, i.e. 65 per cent down to 59.3 per cent. We can also see that food cost has risen by £33,000, i.e. £117,000 – £84,000. It could be suggested that food cost should only have increased by £16,625, i.e. £100,625 – £ 84,000, because we expect it to remain at 35 per cent of sales. This would, however, depend on the restaurant sales mix remaining unchanged and this may not be the case.

To get a better understanding of how the results occurred we require more information. We would be interested to know the level of gross profit we should have achieved from the higher sales volume. To determine this we need to know the budgeted and actual sales mix of the menu items (dishes). We have already received the budgeted and actual number of covers, 20,000 and 25,000 respectively, but this alone may mask a change in the menu item sales mix. The menu sales mix details are, therefore, given in the fixed and flexible budgets shown in Figure 9.5.

The fixed budget is so called because its amounts don't change. It is in fact the annual master budget that once drawn up is not adjusted or altered, regardless of any changes in volume or costs that may occur during the budget period. The flexible budget provides the explanatory link between the fixed budget and the actual results. It can be flexed (adjusted) to take account of the actual level of sales volume achieved. The flexible budget is based on a knowledge of how revenue and costs should behave at a given level of sales volume.

Changes due to sales volume

Referring to Figure 9.5, we can see that the sales value of the actual number of covers sold should be £300,000, i.e. 25,000 × £12 average spend (the average spend was obtained by £240,000 ÷ 20,000). If the actual sales mix of menu items is known we can determine the gross profit that should be

Number of covers	Fixed budget [20,000] (Budgeted sales mix)				Flexible budget [25,000] (Actual sales mix)			
Menu item	Sales mix %	Sales value £	GP %	Gross profit £	Sales mix %	Sales value £	GP %	Gross profit £
1	10	24,000	80	19,200	10	30,000	80	24,000
2	30	72,000	50	36,000	50	150,000	50	75,000
3	50	120,000	75	90,000	30	90,000	75	67,500
4	10	24,000	45	10,800	10	30,000	45	13,500
	100	240,000	65	156,000	100	300,000	60	180,000

£24,000(F)

F = Favourable variance

Figure 9.5 The Acorn Restaurant
Fixed and flexible budgets

achieved. This figure is £180,000 and is obtained by calculating the sales value of each item in the sales mix and multiplying it by the appropriate budgeted gross profit percentage, i.e. (300,000 × 0.1) × 0.8 for item 1, and so on. Thus, the £24,000 favourable variance is the difference between the gross profit obtained from the actual sales volume in the actual sales mix and the budgeted sales volume in the budgeted sales mix. This variance is called the 'sales margin (gross profit) volume variance' because it is the margin that results from a change in the volume of sales, assuming selling prices and food cost are as budgeted. The term 'margin' in this context refers to gross profit as it is the causes of the changes in the gross profit that we are considering.

Changes due to sales quantity and mix

Our analysis in Figure 9.5 provides useful information because it shows us the gross profit expected from the higher sales volume. However, we know that two components are present in the sales margin volume variance, namely the quantity of covers sold which increased from 20,000 to 25,000 and the change in the mixture of sales. What we don't know is the extent to which each component affected gross profit. To determine this we need to add an additional column to our analyses in Figure 9.5 and this is presented in Figure 9.6.

The additional column represents the gross profit that should be achieved if the increase in sales volume had been spread evenly over the menu items, i.e. if the increase in sales had been in the budgeted mix. The figures in the additional column are determined by increasing each menu item gross profit by the percentage increase in sales, or by simply increasing the total gross profit, as follows:

$$\text{Percentage increase in sales} = \frac{£300{,}000}{£240{,}000}$$

$$= 25 \text{ per cent}$$

Number of covers		Fixed budget [20,000] (Budget sales mix)			Flexible budget [25,000] (Budget sales mix)	Flexible budget [25,000] (Actual sales mix)			
Menu item	Sales mix %	Sales value £	GP %	Gross profit £	Gross profit £	Sales mix%	Sale value £	GP %	Gross profit £
1	10	24,000	80	19,200	24,000	10	30,000	80	24,000
2	30	72,000	50	36,000	45,000	50	150,000	50	75,000
3	50	120,000	75	90,000	112,500	30	90,000	75	67,500
4	10	24,000	45	10,800	13,500	10	30,000	45	13,500
	100	240,000	65	156,000	195,000	100	300,000	60	180,000

£39,000(F) £15,000(U)

£24,000(F)

F = Favourable variance
U = Unfavourable variance

Figure 9.6 The Acorn Restaurant
Fixed and flexible budgets

Menu item	£	£
1	19,200 × 1.25 =	24,000
2	36,000 × 1.25 =	45,000
3	90,000 × 1.25 =	112,500
4	10,800 × 1.25 =	13,500
	156,000 × 1.25 =	195,000

Hence, the increase in gross profit due to the higher sales volume, assuming the sales mix remains in the budget proportions, is £39,000 favourable, i.e. £195,000 – £156,000, and is called the 'sales margin quantity variance'. However, because of the change in the actual sales mix the gross profit has reduced, resulting in a 'sales margin mix variance' of £15,000 unfavourable, i.e. £180,000 – £195,000. This has been caused by the lower proportion of sales of menu item 3.

Thus, in summary, the extra gross profit generated from the additional quantity of sales has been offset by the unfavourable change in menu sales mix.

Changes due to selling price and food cost

So far we have concentrated on the control of sales volume, quantity and mix on gross profit. All our comparisons have been based on the assumption that selling prices and food cost remain as budgeted. This, of course, is not often the case and so we need to determine whether we are achieving our budgeted prices and food cost targets.

Referring back to Figure 9.4, the summary results of the Acorn Restaurant show the actual sales revenue generated and food cost incurred, giving an actual gross profit of £170,500 for the budget period. As the flexible budget allows us to determine what our sales and costs should be, we can compare these with those actually achieved, as presented in Figure 9.7.

The actual sales we achieved are lower than the sales we should have generated, resulting in an unfavourable 'selling price variance' of £12,500, i.e. £287,500 – £300,000. This indicates that our budgeted menu prices have been reduced, perhaps to attract additional customers. However, our food cost is less than budget so we have a favourable 'food cost variance' of £3,000, i.e. £117,000 – £120,000, suggesting our overall control of food is satisfactory. The combined effect of these two variances is to decrease expected gross profit, based on actual sales, by £9,500, i.e. £170,500 – £180,000. While the food cost variance is relatively insignificant, the selling price variance should be monitored as price level has a significant influence on profit.

	Flexible budget	Actual results	Variances
Number of covers	25,000 (Actual sales mix)	25,000 (Actual sales mix)	
	£	£	£
Sales revenue	300,000	287,500	12,500(U)
Less: food cost	120,000	117,000	3,000(F)
Gross profit	180,000	170,500	9,500(U)

£9,500(U)

F = Favourable variance
U = Unfavourable variance

Figure 9.7 The Acorn Restaurant
Fixed and flexible budgets: variances

An overview of flexible budget variances

Having analysed our initial restaurant results we can summarize the flexible budget variances in order to see the total picture, illustrated in Figure 9.8.

We can now see at a glance the numerous variances that cause the overall favourable change of £14,500 in budgeted gross profit. If we present the variances in the form of a more readable management report they would appear as in Figure 9.9.

Referring to the budget report in Figure 9.9, and assuming other factors remained constant, we can draw the following conclusions:

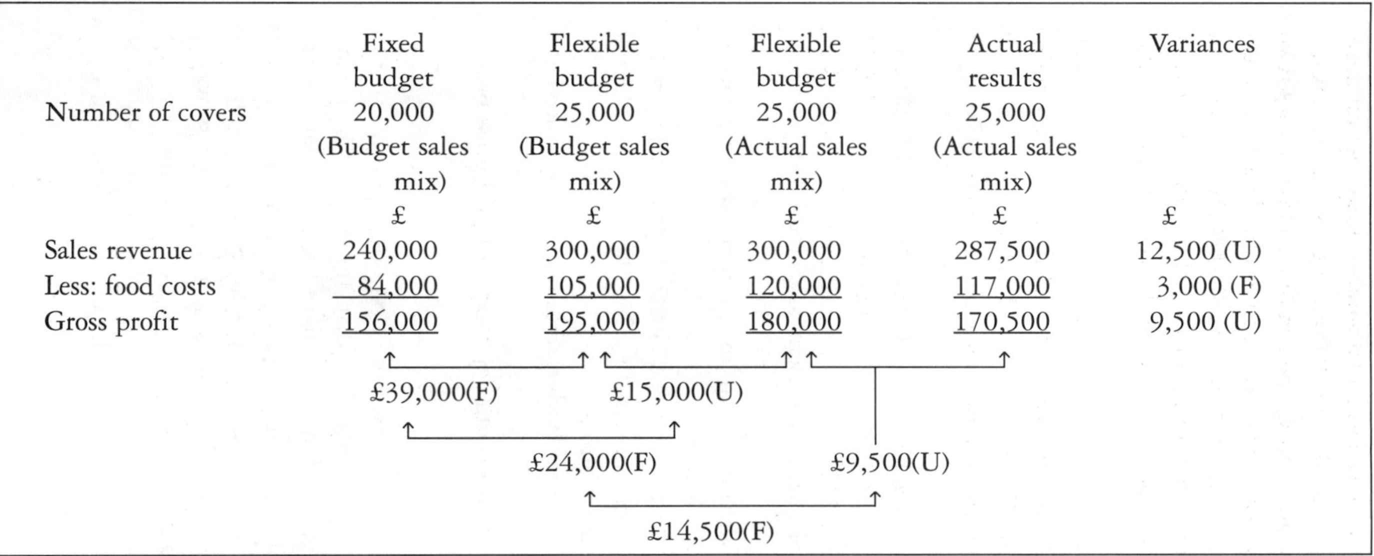

	Fixed budget	Flexible budget	Flexible budget	Actual results	Variances
Number of covers	20,000 (Budget sales mix)	25,000 (Budget sales mix)	25,000 (Actual sales mix)	25,000 (Actual sales mix)	
	£	£	£	£	£
Sales revenue	240,000	300,000	300,000	287,500	12,500 (U)
Less: food costs	84,000	105,000	120,000	117,000	3,000 (F)
Gross profit	156,000	195,000	180,000	170,500	9,500 (U)

Figure 9.8 The Acorn Restaurant Variances

	£	£
Budgeted gross profit for the period		156,000
Sales margin quantity variance	39,000(F)	
Sales margin mix variance	15,000(U)	
Sales margin volume variance	24,000(F)	
Selling price variance	12,500(U)	11,500(F)
		167,500
Food cost variance		3,000(F)
Actual gross profit for the period		£170,500

Figure 9.9 The Acorn Restaurant. Budget report

1 The additional quantity of menu sales increased gross profit by £39,000.
2 The change in the pattern of menu item sales (mix) eroded gross profit by £15,000.
3 The combined effect of the additional quantity and mix of sales improved gross profit by £24,000 i.e. giving the sales margin volume variance.
4 The overall lower than budgeted selling prices reduced gross profit by £12,500.
5 The favourable expenditure on food increased gross profit by £3,000.

The results should be assessed with care. It is possible that the variances are interrelated rather than unrelated. For instance, the increase in sales volume may have been stimulated by the reduction in dish selling prices. This in turn could have attracted customers who selected the lower margin dishes. The food cost variance may be favourable because of less wastage and better discounts due to the increase in volume. Whatever the case, with the intimate knowledge of our own operation the variances will provide a sound basis for understanding and improving future profitability.

10 Using computer spreadsheets

As we have seen earlier, an essential task performed by managers is the planning of future business activities. Among other things this may involve identifying potential markets and developing suitable products and services to satisfy demand, or perhaps consolidating the current share of an existing market. Whatever the case, planning is critical if our business is to remain competitive and profitable.

Having selected the proposed course of action to be pursued this is translated into monetary terms for the purpose of establishing the annual budget. Sales revenue and associated costs are estimated in order to ascertain whether or not the plan is acceptable.

In a case where our initial plan indicates an indequate financial return we will usually wish to know how profit would subsequently respond to changes in particular revenue and cost components. For instance, how will profit be affected if selling price is reduced by 10 per cent? What is the likely effect of this on demand and how does the combined effect of these possible changes influence profit? Until recently, the answers to these and other similar questions could only be determined by laborious calculation and recalculation of the various revenue and cost items in the original budget. However, with developments in computer technology and the widespread availability of electronic spreadsheets these 'what if' kinds of question raised by managers can be answered with greater ease and effectiveness than was previously possible. By using a standard computer spreadsheet package it is possible for us to design and build an effective model that facilitates the routine financial planning requirements of a particular undertaking.

The aim of this chapter is, therefore, three-fold: first, to show how a simple financial model can be created and tested; second, to outline the essentials of spreadsheet design and relate the principles to the simple model; and finally, to incorporate the design principles into a simulated restaurant business broadly following the format recommended in the Uniform System of Accounts for Restaurants.

A brief review of the electronic spreadsheet

An electronic spreadsheet takes the form of a large grid which comprises columns and rows where labels and mathematical values are keyed in and processed with the aid of a computer. Once the spreadsheet programme is loaded, labels, values and formulas can be entered at any point on the grid. This is similar to entering words and numbers on accounting analysis paper. The difference is that the spreadsheet allows formulas to be entered and then if a value is changed the computer facilitates the recalculation of the associated values via the appropriate formulas.

From our viewpoint as a user the major benefits derived from the implementation of a spreadsheet package are as follows:

- *Absence of programming.* We can develop a spreadsheet model without the knowledge of how to program. The command structure of the particular package has to be learned, but most of the packages are similar in principle and relatively straightforward to operate.
- *Rapid computation.* A key feature of the spreadsheet is the speed at which the program calculates data. For instance, values can be changed in a profit statement and the new position calculated within a few seconds – a powerful facil-

ity when considering the different options available to managers.

- *Instant feed back*. As numerical or mathematical data is entered in a spreadsheet the rapid computation provides an instantaneous result. If a result is unrealistic then the error will usually become apparent.
- *Flexibility*. If the spreadsheet is required to be adapted the rows and columns can easily be manipulated to facilitate a new and improved layout.
- *Documentation*. When the spreadsheet model is created it can be printed out (hard copy) and retained for easy reference.
- *Data presentation*. Many spreadsheet programs not only allow the numerical layout to be viewed on screen and hard copied, but in addition will facilitate the display of the formulas in the same configuration. This makes interpretation of the model simpler for other readers.

Creating a simple financial model

In order to explain the fundamentals of building a financial model the assumed data for a restaurant, given in Figure 10.1, will be used.

Restaurant A	
Number of covers	30,000
Selling price per cover	£10
Variable cost per cover	£3
Fixed costs for the period	£180,000

Figure 10.1 Annual budget summary

Stage 1

The first step to be taken in building the model is to decide on an appropriate layout of the financial information. From an accounting standpoint the data may ideally be presented in the form of a marginal cost (or contribution margin) statement. The annual budget data for Restaurant A can be entered on to the spreadsheet grid by typing in the relevant labels and values, as per Figure 10.2(a). The break-even point in terms of the number of covers has been included on the grid as it is an important intermediate target for the restaurant to achieve. At this stage the spreadsheet is not a model because it does not contain the formulas which form the mathematical relationships between the separate decision variables (items of data that could change).

Stage 2

The next step, therefore, is to enter the formulas for Restaurant A thereby creating the spreadsheet model. This is effected by selecting a value from the spreadsheet and deciding on a formula that will give the result. For instance, £300,000 sales revenue in cell B5 was determined by 30,000 covers × £10 selling price per cover, i.e. cells B2*C5. The formula may now be entered at cell B5 along with formulas appropriate to other cells on the grid (see Figure 10.2(b)). The formulas do not normally appear visually on the screen in their respective cell positions. They are stored in the computer memory, but will appear on the cell indicator line when the cursor is moved on to a cell that contains a formula. Note that as it is not possible to display a value and a formula simultaneously in a cell, Figure 10.2(b) and other similar figures show the formulas separately. Essentially, however, the formulas sit unseen in their respective cells.

The two fundamental steps to building a financial model, depicted in Figures 10.2(a) and 10.2(b), assist the first-time user in relating accounting principles to the mechanics of the spreadsheet. Theoretically, however, the first step of entering the given accounting data (Figure 10.2(a)) can be omitted. Instead, it is possible to build the spreadsheet model directly by typing in labels and formulas at the outset (Figure 10.2(b)). However, by entering the values, such as the £300,000 sales revenue, prior to entering the formula provides a useful check on the accuracy of the formula. If the formula is correct then the £300,000 will not change. On the other hand, if the value does change the formula is likely to contain an error and should be checked. Once this is completed the decision variables, i.e. number of covers, selling price per cover, fixed costs, etc., can be added to the spreadsheet and the computer will then calculate the appropriate profit and break-even point.

Stage 3

Thus, by whichever means, having created the spreadsheet model by the final step is to test that it is working correctly. Using the restaurant model this can be effected by changing each decision variable in turn and observing the effect on profit and break-even position: for instance, increase the number of covers sold from 30,000 to 40,000. The computer should recalculate the position to show a new net profit of £100,000, an increase of £70,000 on the previous profit. The break-even point is, of course, not affected by changes in numbers of products sold. Another check would be to increase the fixed costs from £180,000 to £210,000. This should have the effect of reducing net profit from £30,000 to zero and increasing the break-even point from 25,715 to 30,000 covers. Hence, assuming each change in a decision variable results in the correct outcome in the appropriate formula cells, the spreadsheet can be judged to be working correctly. The restaurant's management can now try out various 'what if?' situations and evaluate the subsequent effects on sales, costs and profit.

Designing a spreadsheet

Creating a spreadsheet model such as the one presented in Figures 10.2(a) and 10.2(b) is fairly straightforward because it fits within a single computer VDU (visual display unit) screen, i.e. the model does not extent beyond 6–8 columns in width or 20–30 rows in depth. However, in practice this is rarely the case as the model is more likely to extend over several screens thus preventing the user from viewing it all at the same time.

In order to build a larger spreadsheet model a more formal approach to spreadsheet design is required that will reduce the possibility of errors and facilitate a logical and well-organized

(a)

	A	B	C
1	Model 1	Rest	A
2	No. covers sold	30000	Cover
3		———	———
4		£	£
5	Sales revenue	300000	10
6	Less: Variable costs	90000	3
7		———	———
8	Contribution margin	210000	7
9			═══
10	Less: Fixed costs	180000	
11		———	
12	Net profit/loss	30000	
13		═══	
14			
15	BEP in covers	25715	
16			
17			17

(b)

	A	B	C
1	Model 1	Rest	A
2	No. covers sold	30000	Cover
3		———	———
4		£	£
5	Sales revenue	+B2*C5	10
6	Less: Variable costs	+B2*C6	3
7		———	———
8	Contribution margin	+B5–B6	+C5–C6
9			═══
10	Less: Fixed costs	180000	
11		———	
12	Net profit/loss	+B8–B10	
13		═══	
14			
15	BEP in covers	+B10/C8	
16			

Note commas are added to the sterling values using a format command, explained later.

Figure 10.2 (a) Spreadsheet grid (showing values) (b) Spreadsheet grid (showing formulas)

series of entries and presentation of data. To this end a number of principles and guidelines have evolved that form the basis for the effective design of a working spreadsheet model. The main ones are explained below:

1 Prepare the initial spreadsheet model design on paper

Understandably, we usually want to design a spreadsheet model straight on to a computer. This, however, often proves to be a difficult and onerous task which results in error and frustration. It can be overcome by preparing the initial outline draft of the model on paper away from the computer. This will provide an overview of the model that can draw attention to what may otherwise be unforeseeable problems. In the long run a paper design will probably save time and assist in the development of a more efficient model.

2 Identify grid areas as input and output screens

An input screen is an area that contains items (decision variables) that could change when the model is in use, e.g. covers sold, average spend per cover, food cost percentage of sales revenue. Input screens can contain cell references and formulas if required. An output screen is an area where all entries from other areas of the spreadsheet are referenced and calculated. Thus, input screens mainly contain decision variables and output screens only contain references and formulas.

3 Enter a decision variable directly only once

The value of each decision variable should be typed directly into an input screen cell once only. If the cell value is also required in another part of the spreadsheet model then follow principle (4) below.

4 Move between input and output screens by cell reference only

If a decision variable cell value or formula cell value is required elsewhere in a spreadsheet model it should be entered by reference to the particular cell address. For example, assume that the number of covers sold for the first quarter of the year is entered in cell B4 on the input screen.

If this figure is required on an output screen at cell B55 then the notation B4 is entered at cell B55. Therefore, if the number of covers sold is altered at cell B4 the change will automatically be reflected at cell B55.

5 *Where practicable build input and output screens with parallel structures*

For instance, if column C represents the second quarter of the year in an input screen then it should also represent the second quarter in subsequent output screens. This will enable other users to follow the logic of the model more easily.

6 *Never include a decision variable in a formula*

This is a crucial principle. For example, if the cost of sales is 40 per cent of sales revenue the formula could be entered as B44*0.4 at the appropriate cell (the B44 being the sales revenue figure reference from the input screen). However, this would mean that any cells containing the cost of sales percentage would have to be identified each time the percentage is changed. The effect would be to destroy the logic of the model. The correct approach is to enter 0.4 at cell (say) B12 in the input screen and multiply the two cells together by entering B44*B12 at a third cell in the output screen.

7 *Include a summary of results screen*

In the case of large and more complex models it is sometimes desirable, though not essential, to create an output screen that contains key 'bottom-line' results that can be viewed on a single screen. For example, if a profit planning model comprises a quarterly cash budget and profit statement, it might be helpful to view the net impact of all changes in decision variables on profits, cash balances and break-even thresholds on one screen. For ease of access the results screen is usually best located in close proximity to the input screen.

8 *Incorporate appropriate instructions in the spreadsheet model*

Again, this is dependent on the complexity of the model. For example, it may be useful to explain how to enter data on the screen. Also, where the model extends over a large area of the spreadsheet grid it may be appropriate to include a table of contents with grid references in order for users to identify and locate the various input and output screens.

9 Test the spreadsheet model for proper functioning

Clearly, the extent of testing will depend on the size and complexity of the model, but manual checks should be made before using it. For instance, change selected decision variables and check that the results are consistent with the changes.

In order to illustrate the effect building a financial model that incorporates the appropriate spreadsheet design principles discussed above, the simple Restaurant A model has been reconstructed and presented in Figure 10.3(a) and (b).

Notice the model input and output screens have been identified on the grid, but that due to its small size both screens are able to be displayed on a single computer VDU screen. However, as illustrated later, for larger models the input and output screen will usually take up grid space equivalent to several VDU screens which will prevent a complete model being viewed at one time.

Note in particular that our redesign shows that the input screen contains only decision variables, i.e. items that could change, while the output screen contains only formulas. Although the values in the cells which contain formulas will change, if the input screen variables are adjusted the formulas themselves remain unchanged.

All movements between screens follow the cell reference principle and the screens have been built with parallel structures, i.e. input decision variables and output formulas follow through under column B. Also, formula cells do not contain any decision variables. Testing of the model should indicate correct functioning.

Spreadsheet graphics

In addition to facilitating the creation of financial models, spreadsheet packages normally include a graphics option. This allows us

(a)

	A	:B	: C :
1	Model 2		
2	INPUT SCREEN	Rest. A	
3	Number of covers sold	30000	
4	Selling price per cover (£)	10	
5	Variable cost per cover (£)	3	
6	Fixed costs (£)	180000	
7			
8	OUTPUT SCREEN	£	
9	Sales revenue	300000	
10	Less: Variable costs	90000	
11		——	
12	Contribution margin	210000	
13	Less: Fixed costs	180000	
14		——	
15	Net profit/loss	30000	
16		═════	
17			
18	BEP in covers	25715	

(b)

	A	: B	: C :
1	Model 2		
2	INPUT SCREEN	Rest. A	
3	Number of covers sold	30000	
4	Selling price per cover (£)	10	
5	Variable cost per cover (£)	3	
6	Fixed costs (£)	180000	
7			
8	OUTPUT SCREEN		
9	Sales revenue	+B3*B4	
10	Less: Variable costs	+B3*B5	
11		——	
12	Contribution margin	+B9–B10	
13	Less: Fixed costs	+B6	
14		——	
15	Net profit/loss	+B12–B13	
16		═════	
17			
18	BEP in covers	+B6/(B4–B5)	

Input and output screens appear on one VDU screen due to the small size of the model.

Figure 10.3 (a) Spreadsheet grid (showing values) (b) Spreadsheet grid (showing formulas)

to display a graphical representation of results drawn from a particular model. For example, a manager may wish to view a break-even graph of a restaurant so as to gain an overall perspective of the cost structure and potential profits and losses at various levels of sales. To illustrate this the Restaurant A model in Figure 10.3 has been modified, as shown in Figure 10.4, and presented in the form of a break-even graph in Figure 10.5.

A spreadsheet program produces a CVP graph in a manner similar to a graph drawn manually. The graphics option is usually based on a linear model and therefore the program will require two pieces of data in order to draw each straight line. To facilitate that it is necessary to introduce a second set of data for the Restaurant A example, shown in Figure 10.4. The additional set of data entered is based on zero sales and thus provides a range of activity for the program to draw the break-even graph presented in Figure 10.5. Note that 'total costs' have been added to the model in order to allow the program to draw the total cost line on the graph.

Once the CVP graph has been created any changes made to the decision variables in the input screen will not only adjust the sales, costs and profit in the output screen, but will also adjust the graph to reflect the changes. Thus the effect of a variety of financial decisions can be displayed and evaluated on screen in both numerical and graphical forms.

Developing a restaurant model

Having considered an approach to designing and building a simple financial model the principles and methods can readily be applied to the creation of larger and more practical models relating to the hospitality industry. In order, therefore, to follow on from the earlier discussion, an annual profit planning model for an assumed restaurant business has been developed and is presented in Figure 10.6.

Examination of Figure 10.6 reveals that in this case the larger number of decision variables in the input screen completely fills a VDU screen. Also, the increased financial detail required with respect to sales, costs and profits necessitates the use of two output screens to contain the data. Thus, the restaurant model

(a)

	A	B	C
1	Model 3		
2	INPUT SCREEN	Rest. A	Rest. A
3	Number of covers sold	0	30000
4	Selling price per cover (£)	10	10
5	Variable cost per cover (£)	3	3
6	Fixed costs (£)	180000	180000
7			
8	OUTPUT SCREEN	£	£
9	Sales revenue	0	300000
10	Less: Variable costs	0	90000
11		——	——
12	Contribution margin	0	210000
13	Less: Fixed costs	180000	180000
14		——	——
15	Net profit/loss	–180000	30000
16		══════	══════
17	Total costs	180000	270000
18	BEP in covers		25715

(b)

	A	B	C
1	Model 3		
2	INPUT SCREEN	Rest. A	Rest. A
3	Number of covers sold	0	30000
4	Selling price per cover (£)	10	10
5	Variable cost per cover (£)	3	3
6	Fixed costs (£)	180000	180000
7			
8	OUTPUT SCREEN	£	£
9	Sales revenue	+ B3*B4	+ C3*C4
10	Less: Variable costs	+B3*B5	+C3*C5
11		——	——
12	Contribution margin	+ B9–B10	+ C9–C10
13	Less: Fixed costs	+ B6	+ C6
14		——	——
15	Net profit/loss	+ B12–B13	+ C12–C13
16		══════	══════
17	Total costs	+B10+B13	+C10+C13
18	BEP in covers		+ C6/(C4–C5)

Input and output screens appear on one VDU screen due to the small size of the model.

Figure 10.4 (a) Spreadsheet grid (showing values)
(b) Spreadsheet grid (showing formulas)

extends in total over three full screens. It is worth noting at this point that for still larger models an effort should be made to minimize the number of input screens as it is these that managers will wish constantly to view during their planning sessions.

The profit planning model illustrated in Figure 10.6 is based on the cost–volume–profit analysis (CVP) technique and so the decision variables in the input screen are separated into their fixed and variable components. The estimated fixed components relating to sales revenue and costs are entered as absolute annual amounts, while the variable cost components are entered as percentages of the relevant sales items, as depicted under column E. This facilitates variations in sales, costs and profits, reflected in the output screens, which are prompted by changes in decision variables.

The output screens have consciously been designed in the form of an accounting profit statement which broadly conforms to the Uniform System of Accounts for Restaurants. This is important because whether viewed on screen or as a printed hard copy, outputs are more easily read and evaluated if they relate to the needs of the user – in this case restaurant management. The fixed and variable classification of revenue and costs

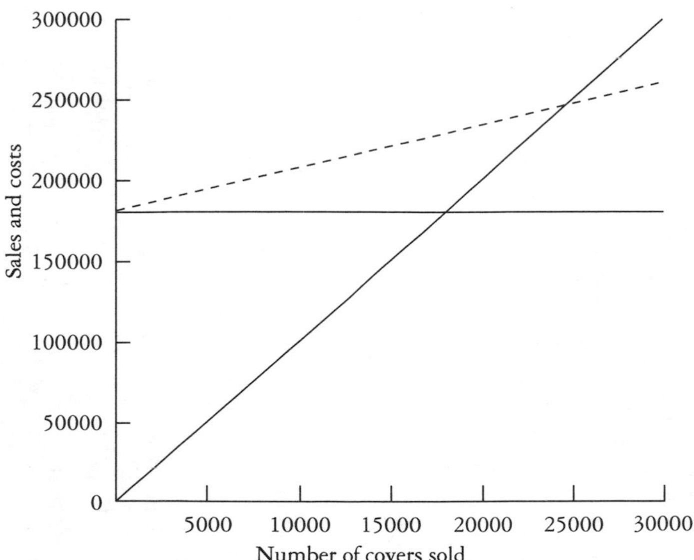

Figure 10.5 Restaurant A: break-even graph

	A	B	C	D	E	F
1	Model 4a			Classification		
2	INPUT SCREEN: Decision variables			Fixed	Variable	
3	Number of covers				20000	
4	Average spend: food			–	6.5	per cover
5	Average spend: beverage			–	3	per cover
6	Shop and public room rental			5000	15000	
7	Cost of sales %: food			–	0.4	food sales
8	Cost of sales %: beverage			–	0.5	beverage sales
9	Payroll and related			25500	0.15	total sales
10	Music and entertainment			6800	–	"
11	Laundry			2000	0.01	"
12	China, glass, linen, etc.			1000	0.005	"
13	Paper supplies			–	0.005	"
14	Menus, printing, etc.			1700	–	
15	Admin. and general			8500	–	
16	Marketing			4000	0.02	F & B sales
17	Repairs and maintenance			3900	0.004	total sales
18	Energy			3800	0.008	"
19	Fixed charges			22500	–	
20						
21	OUTPUT SCREEN 1: sales, gross profit and rental income					
22		Annual		Classification		
23		amounts		Fixed	Variable	
24	Sales revenue:	£		£	£	
25	Food	130000		–	130000	
26	Beverage	600000		–	600000	
27		———				
28	Total	190000				
29		———				
30	Cost of sales:					
31	Food	52000		–	52000	
32	Beverage	30000		–	30000	
33		———				

34	Total	82000		
35		———		
36	Gross profit	108000		
37	Shop and public room rental	20000	5000	15000
38		———		
39	Total income	128000		
40		———		
41	OUTPUT SCREEN 2: expenses, fixed charges and profits			
42	Controllable expenses:	£	£	£
43	Payroll and related	54000	25500	28500
44	Music and entertainment	6800	6800	–
45	Laundry	3900	2000	1900
46	China, glass, linen, etc.	1950	1000	950
47	Paper supplies	950	–	950
48	Menus, printing, etc.	1700	1700	–
49	Admin and general	8500	8500	–
50	Marketing	7800	4000	3800
51	Repairs and maintenance	4600	3900	760
52	Energy	5320	3800	1520
53		———		
54	Total	95580		
55		———		
56	Profit before fixed charges	32420		
57	Fixed charges	22500	22500	–
58		———		
59	Net profit or loss	9920		
60		———		

Figure 10.6 Restaurant model (showing values)

	A	B	C	D	E	F
21	OUTPUT SCREEN 1: sales, gross profit and rental income					
22		Annual		Classification		
23		amounts		Fixed	Variable	
24	Sales revenue:	£		£	£	
25	Food	+E25		–	+E3*E4	
26	Beverage	+E26		–	+E3*E5	
27		———				
28	Total	+B25+B26				
29		———				
30	Cost of sales:					
31	Food	+E31		–	+E25*E7	
32	Beverage	+E32		–	+B26*E8	
33		———				
34	Total	+B31+B32				
35		———				
36	Gross profit	+B28–B34				
37	Shop and public room rental	+D37+E37		+D6	+E6	
38		———				
39	Total income	+B36+B37				
40		———				
41	OUTPUT SCREEN 2: expenses, fixed charges and profits					
42	Controllable expenses:	£		£	£	
43	Payroll and related	+D43+E43		+D9	+B28*E9	

44	Music and entertainment	+D10	+D10	–
45	Laundry	+D45+E45	+D11	+B28*E11
46	China, glass, linen, etc.	+D46+E46	+D12	+B28*E12
47	Paper supplies	+E47	–	+B28*E13
48	Menus, printing, etc.	+D48	+D14	–
49	Admin. and general	+D49	+D15	–
50	Marketing	+D50 +E50	+D16	(B25+B26)*E16
51	Repairs and maintenance	+D51 +E51	+D17	+B28*E17
52	Energy	+D52+E52	+D18	+B28*E18
53		________		
54	Total	@SUM (B43. .B52)		
55		________		
56	Profit before fixed charges	+B39–B54		
57	Fixed charges	+D57	+D19	–
58		________		
59	Net profit or loss	+B56–B57		
60		________		

Figure 10.7 Restaurant model: output screens (showing formulas)

in the input screen has been carried through to the output screens in order for management to be able to assess the magnitude of the figures in absolute (money) terms.

As mentioned earlier, most spreadsheet packages have the facility to display and print formulas in the same configuration as the layout of the model. Reference to Figure 10.7 shows the formulas in the two output screens (the input screen remains the same as in Figure 10.6) and thus enables the user to understand, review and, if necessary, amend the model as appropriate. Furthermore, it can be seen that the restaurant model adheres to the relevant design principles discussed earlier.

With regard to improving the screen and printed copy presentation of the model a format command could be used. This allows sterling amounts in cells to be prefixed with the pound (£) sign, commas to be included in the figures, and percentage signs where percentages are relevant. Note, however, that if these refinements are not entered using the format command the programme will interpret the particular cells as labels (words) and be unable to use them for computation purposes.

An important point to bear in mind is that, during the process of building a model, the user should save the data on screen at regular intervals of 15–30 minutes in case of power failure or some other unforeseen occurrence. Finally, after each building session the model should be copied on to a back-up disk to ensure that a spare copy is always available in the event of the initial disk being mislaid, damaged or corrupted.

Spreadsheet applications

Once the fundamentals of spreadsheet design and construction have been understood the principles can be applied to a wide variety of financial planning and control situations faced by managers. These include cost–volume–profit analysis, routine rooms, food and beverage budgeting, flexible budgetary control, comparative analysis, stock control, credit management, cash forecasting, menu engineering, profit sensitivity analysis, budget variance comparisons, market share analysis, pricing decisions, and so on. Spreadsheets do not have to be large and complex to be effective. If a model is logically designed and built with care it will prove a powerful aid to management decision making.

11 Getting the information we need

Why do we need financial information?

Information is essential to all managers if we are to be effective. If we consider any management function, such as planning, organizing, or controlling, we need information in order to make informed decisions.

We are all involved in decision making; we have to make choices when alternatives exist. The choice may be simply between taking action and not taking action in a given situation, but we would need to consider the benefits of each alternative. It would be difficult for us to be effective without utilizing information to aid the decision-making process.

It is simple to say we need information, but the practicalities of determining the appropriate information are not so straightforward:

- What is information?
- What volume is most useful?
- Is the information relevant to the situation?
- Does the user understand the information?

- Did the information arrive in time to be useful?

If we are to receive and give others good quality information that aids the decision making process these questions need to be considered.

What is information?

Anything that adds to the knowledge of the receiver is information. Information is data that has been processed into a form that is meaningful and relevant to the user (Figure 11.1).

In all operations there are numerous financial data. What we are concerned with is processing the data in such a way that it becomes useful information to the user. In order to do this we must understand the characteristics of good quality information. Information should be:

- accurate;
- in an understandable form;
- of suitable frequency;

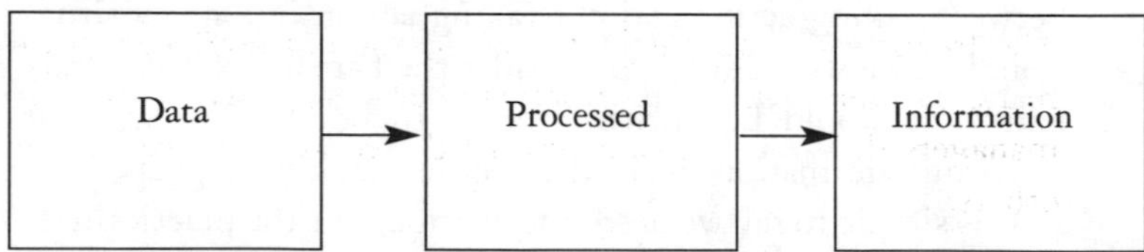

Figure 11.1 Source of information

- of right breadth;
- of authoritative origin;
- relevant;
- complete;
- in time to be of use.

Accurate

Accuracy is important – if we make a decision based on inaccurate information the results could be dangerous. It rests with the provider of the information to make sure it is accurate before it is communicated.

In an understandable form

Financial information can be numerically or graphically communicated, for instance through cost–volume–profit graphs, bar graphs, line diagrams and pie charts. We can communicate information in many ways, for example through word of mouth, in printed form, or on a computer screen. We must consider that a summary form might be appropriate in one situation, but a full report in another.

Frequency

The frequency with which the information is produced must relate to users' needs. Information that is reported to certain managers daily may only be required weekly, or monthly, by others.

Breadth

Too often companies ignore the importance of the breadth of information and produce standard reports to go to various managers. These may not relate directly to the managers' span of control. A unit manager needs a report giving details of the individual unit, while an area manager may require the same details for many units in one report.

Authoritative origin

Information can come from many internal and external sources. It is important that we feel comfortable with the origin of the information, i.e. we believe it is reliable and valid.

Relevant

Information has to be relevant to the current situation. As the situation changes the information should be reviewed in order to ensure it remains relevant.

Complete

Information provides us with knowledge in order that we might make decisions. Unless the information is complete, decisions are made with a degree of conjecture. It is essential that the information should be as complete as possible.

In time to be of use

Timeliness of information is essential. Information that arrives after the decision has been made is of little use!

In the hospitality industry the sources of raw data are vast. Computerized reservation and accounting systems have significantly increased access to internal data. As we saw earlier, data and information are different – the availability of raw data does not always lead to the supply of good quality information.

It is important that the attributes mentioned above are considered when we contemplate information requirements. Information should focus on the key aspects associated with our management roles.

The above are the ingredients for useful information, but where do we start in planning a financial information system that will give us this information?

The base of an information system

There are many places to start when reviewing or setting up an information system. We need to consider the effects of using certain bases and make sure we start at the right point. Remember to consider these from the point of view of both the giver and the receiver of information. Management reports should be market driven in that they should relate to the needs of the user.

The system

In the short term the existing system may restrict the frequency and type of information available. When we are reviewing a system we should not feel restricted by what the system can do in the short-term.

The accountant

In many operations the source of data for most information is the accountant. If the accountant is left to determine what information we need the information may be accounting and not operationally oriented.

The manager's boss

When a more senior manager decides what information an individual should have subjectivity must be considered. We may consider what we would like if employed in that role, or consider what we need to know about that section for our own needs.

The manager's wants

It would seem logical that individuals requiring the information are the best judges of what they want. Our wants may not produce the best information system for several reasons. It may be that as individuals we are unaware that certain information exists or that it could be useful to us if we had it.

The manager's needs

Actual need must be an essential element of any information system. This is easy to justify, but in practice how can we identify needs, as opposed to wants? We can consider the needs of the position and the needs of the individual for financial information. This is a good base to use for reviewing or implementing a financial information system providing we have an effective system to ascertain actual needs.

How can we identify information needs?

A simple solution would be to ask, but would this achieve the right results? When asked, we may identify only information we have used in the past and found useful, thus other potentially useful information of which we are unaware will be omitted. Also, individuals' answers may be influenced by who is asking the question and how they feel they should answer.

An approach that can be used to overcome the problems of asking directly is to consider the position itself, and from that to identify the areas where information is required. This approach considers the 'critical success factors', i.e. the few things that must go right within the business. These are the areas we need to track and, therefore, need information about.

Critical success factors approach

- *Step 1.* Identify goals that exist for the particular position. That is to say the specific targets that we aim to achieve. In management we should all have set goals to achieve, so this step should be straightforward.

- *Step 2*. For each goal identified we then need to determine the critical success factors in meeting the goal. These are the few key areas where things 'must go right' if we are to be successful.
- *Step 3*. Each critical success factor needs to be controlled closely if the goals are to be met. For each critical success factor identified we need to draw up a list of measures.
- *Step 4*. The measures will form the basis for our financial information system. This final step is to decide the raw data we need in the system in order to report on the measures identified.

A simple example would be:

Goal:	To increase rooms revenue by 8 per cent.
CSFs:	The number of rooms sold. The room rate charged.
Measures:	Occupancy percentage achieved, compared with previous period. Average room rate achieved compared with previous period.

In summary the stages are as shown in Figure 11.2. Not only does this approach give us a good base for an information system, it also ensures managers are looking to the future by having clearly defined goals. We are also made to consider the areas that are critical to success in order to achieve the goals set. All too often managers get drawn in to viewing all the financial information available without giving priority to the essential elements that need close attention.

Changing information needs

We have considered how to identify the information needs of managers, but we should not forget that in business our goals do not remain the same. As our goals change our information needs are likely to change. We need to ensure our information system is reviewed at regular intervals.

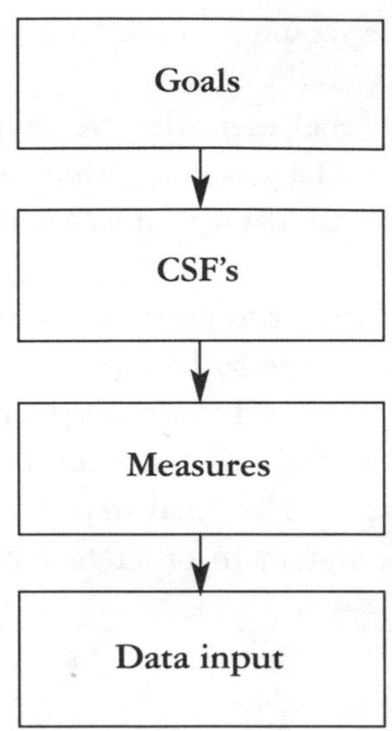

Figure 11.2 Stages to determine information needs

It is good practice to review our aims and goals regularly, and review of our information system can be combined with this. For example, when we set up a new business we may concentrate on obtaining finance for the venture, developing systems and standards, etc. Once a business is up and running the emphasis is likely to change to building up repeat business, developing new markets and maintaining the established standards. In this situation the goal of establishing standards has been achieved, and our next goal may now become maintaining standards. The emphasis of the information we require regarding standards is likely to change as well. For instance, we may monitor this area less frequently.

Initially we may be aiming to develop the volume of business, but when this reaches a certain level efforts may concentrate on increasing average spend, or expansion through increasing the size of the outlet or opening a new unit.

A business moves forward if we are constantly considering progress and looking for new business alternatives and opportunities. Our financial information system can help us to do this providing it is updated and reviewed alongside our goals. Figure 11.3 is an example of a business in trouble, where the management team is seen as a cause for concern

Goal	CSFs	Measures
To improve the level of efficiency and profitability.	Developing the management team to their full potential.	Internal promotion rate.
		Guest feedback.
	Improving guest satisfaction.	Employee surveys.
	Boost staff morale	Level of repeat business.
		Staff training records.

Figure 11.3

Figure 11.3 shows the immediate action required to alleviate an existing problem. Once the management team is strengthened and customers are content with the service offered the goal will change.

If we consider the measures in Figure 11.4 we will see that some are the same as those shown in Figure 11.3, but now there is less emphasis on the management team and greater emphasis on profits.

Goal	CSFs	Measures
To provide a good quality and profitable service.	Guest perception of value.	Guest feedback.
	Guest loyalty.	Level of repeat business.
	Standard of product.	Market share achieved.
	Effective financial controls.	Cash flow. Departmental profit.
		Profit before fixed charges percentage.

Figure 11.4

So, when it is felt that the product and management team are acceptable, attention can be turned to the financial success of the business, while still maintaining product quality.

We started this chapter by stating that information is essential to the decision making process. It is our judgement of the information that makes or breaks a business through our decisions. We rely on good quality information. Quality information can only exist when information needs are clearly defined and reviewed at regular intervals.

12 Capital expenditure decisions

Up to this point we have focused our attention on routine profit-planning methods and techniques that are intended to improve profit on a day-to-day basis over the short term, i.e. usually one year. In this chapter we will concentrate on the longer term, and in particular on those methods that are used to assess capital expenditure.

Examples of decisions that involve capital expenditure include the purchase of new equipment and machinery, extension or refurbishment of existing facilities, and new product development. These are often critical decisions for a business because they normally entail:

- commitment of large sums of money;
- long periods of time;
- irreversible decisions.

Discounted Cash Flow (DCF)

There are several approaches to evaluating capital expenditure decisions, but the most widely accepted method is discounted cash flow. The reason for this is that it recognizes that money has a time value.

Let us consider a simple example to understand the concept. Assuming a rate of interest of 10 per cent per annum then:

(a) £1 invested today will amount to £1.10 in one year's time.
(b) Conversely, the value of £1.10 received in one year's time will be worth £1 today.

If we extend this for a longer period, for instance, five years, the position will appear as in Figure 12.1

(a) Value of £1 at the end of 1 year at 10% is £1.00 + £0.10 = £1.10

£1	2	£1.10 + £0.11 = £1.21
£1	3	£1.21 + £0.12 = £1.33
£1	4	£1.33 + £0.13 = £1.46
£1	5	£1.46 + £0.15 = £1.61

(b) £1 receivable in one year's time is $\frac{£1}{1.1} = £0.909$

£1	2	$\frac{£1}{1.21} = £0.826$
£1	3	$\frac{£1}{1.33} = £0.751$
£1	4	$\frac{£1}{1.46} = £0.683$
£1	5	$\frac{£1}{1.61} = £0.621$

Figure 12.1 The time value of money

From Figure 12.1 we can see that the value of money is directly affected by time and that interest is the method used to express the time value of money. Thus, using our example, if we discount £1, receivable in one year's time, back to today's value we find it is worth £0.909. Again if we discount £1, receivable in two years' time, back to today's value it will be worth £0.826 and so on for the subsequent amounts. We can see this presented diagrammatically in Figure 12.2.

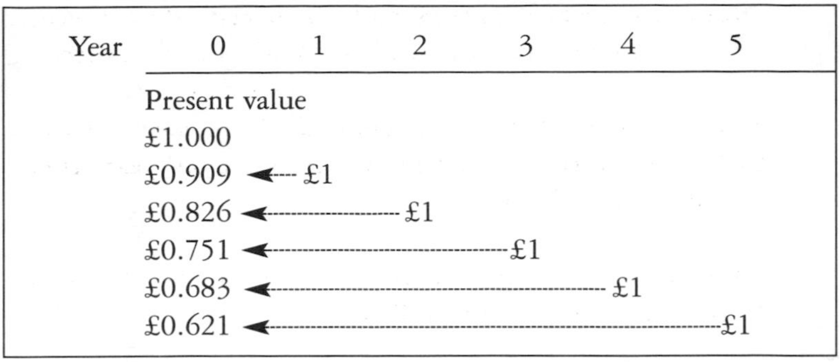

Year	0	1	2	3	4	5
	Present value					
	£1.000					
	£0.909 ←	£1				
	£0.826 ←		£1			
	£0.751 ←			£1		
	£0.683 ←				£1	
	£0.621 ←					£1

Figure 12.2 Future cash flows discounted at 10 per cent back to present-day values

Note that at a discount rate of 10 per cent, £1 received today has a present value of £1, whereas £1 received in five years' time has a present value of £0.621. So the present value of £1 received at the end of five years is calculated as follows:

$£1.00 \times 0.621 = £0.621$

Hence, if we received £10,000 at the end of five years the present value (assuming a 10 per cent rate of interest) will be as follows:

$£10{,}000 \times 0.621 = £6{,}210$

We can prove the result by applying compound interest of 10 per cent to £6,210 over five years, which will give £10,000. The 0.621 acts as a 'factor' (multiplier) which can be used to multiply any amounts of money received five years hence at an interest rate of 10 per cent. Thus, discounted cash flow is simply compound interest in reverse and, therefore, discount factors can be calculated for any level of interest rate required. (To save us the effort of calculation, a discount table is provided at the end of this chapter.) So, having explained the concept of discounted cash flow we can now apply it to an example.

DCF: Net Present Value method

This method is based on an assumed minimum rate of return (discount rate) and we usually use this rate to discount (multi-

Initial capital outlay	£30,000
Estimated project life	5 years
Annual cash flow from operations	£10,000
Required rate of return	10%

Year	Cash inflow	DCF factor at10%	Total present value (0)	1	2	3	4	5
				Cash inflows (years)				
1	£10,000	0.909	£9,090 ←	£10,000				
2	10,000	0.826	8,260 ←		£10,000			
3	10,000	0.751	7,510 ←			£10,000		
4	10,000	0.683	6,830 ←				£10,000	
5	10,000	0.621	6,210 ←					£10,000
Present value of inflows			£37,900					
Initial outlay			30,000					
Net present value			£ 7,900					

Since the present value of the cash flows is greater than the present value of the initial capital outlay the project should be accepted.

Figure 12.3 Net Present Value method: The Wellington Hotel

ply) the future cash flows to their present value. The investment outlay is subtracted from the present value of cash flows, leaving a residual sum which is the net present value. A decision will be made in favour of the project if the Net Present Value (NPV) is a positive figure. We can apply this method to compare one capital expenditure project with another. The project with the higher NPV would be the one selected. Figure 12.3 shows the assumed figures of the Wellington Hotel.

DCF: Internal Rate of Return method (IRR)

This method requires us to calculate the rate of interest that will reduce the net present value of a project to zero. This will enable us to compare the internal rate of return directly with the required rate. Again, using the information in our Wellington Hotel example we can compute the internal rate of return, shown in Figure 12.4.

The internal rate of return for the hotel project is 19.875 per cent. Or stated slightly differently the project would recover the full £30,000 capital outlay and, in addition, earn 9.875 per cent interest. A word of warning though, we should be careful not to place too much emphasis on the precise figure of return as the cash flows are only estimates which may vary substantially over the period of the project's life.

Net Present Value versus Internal Rate of Return

Despite the difference in approach used by the Net Present Value and the Internal Rate of Return methods, they will both always indicate the same 'accept' or 'reject' position for a given project. However, in the case where two projects were being considered and only one could be selected (mutually exclusive) the NPV and IRR rankings may differ. For instance, if a hotel was evaluating two computer reservation systems it would want to accept the most profitable one and reject the other,

Year	Cash inflow	DCF factor at 10%	Total present value	DCF factor at 20%	Total present value
1	£10,000	0.909	£9,090	0.833	£8,330
2	10,000	0.826	8,260	0.694	6,940
3	10,000	0.751	7,510	0.579	5,790
4	10,000	0.683	6,830	0.482	4,820
5	10,000	0.621	6,210	0.402	4,020
Present value of inflows			37,900		29,900
Initial outlay			30,000		30,000
Net present value			£ 7,900		£ (100)

The IRR is calculated as follows:

Differences in DCF rates 20% – 10% = 10%

Difference in NPV £(100) – £7,900 = £8,000

The rate to add to 10% so that NPV = £0 is:

$$\frac{£7,900}{£8,000} \times 10\% = 9.875\%$$

Therefore, the IRR i.e. the true rate is 10% + 9.875% = 19.875%

Figure 12.4 Internal Rate of Return method: The Wellington Hotel

even though the other system was profitable, i.e. the most profitable in this context means the greatest cost saving.

Hence, if we wish to maximize profitability from our investments, there are situations where we will need to rank alternative projects in order of potential profitability. In some instances the NPV and IRR for alternative projects can produce conflicting rankings of potential profitability due to differences in capital outlay or the timing of future cash flows, or both. To illustrate this we will consider two mutually exclusive projects, each with the same initial capital outlay, but with differing amounts and timing of cash flows. First let us determine the NPV of each project, shown in Figure 12.5.

We can see that the NPV ranking, based on a return of 10 per cent, determines our choice to be project. A because its net present value is greater than project B. Now let us determine the IRR of each project, shown in Figure 12.6.

	Project A			Project B		
Year	Cash inflow	DCF factor at 10%	Total present value	Cash inflow	DCF factor at 10%	Total present value
1	£3,000	0.909	£2,727	£6,000	0.909	£5,454
2	3,000	0.826	2,478	5,000	0.826	4,130
3	4,000	0.751	3,004	4,000	0.751	3,004
4	9,000	0.683	6,147	2,000	0.683	1,366
Present value of inflows			14,356			13,954
Initial outlay			10,000			10,000
Net present value			£4,356			£3,954
Ranking per NPV			(1)			(2)

Figure 12.5 Two mutually exclusive projects: Net Present Value ranking

	Project A			Project B		
Year	Cash inflow	DCF factor at 25%	Total present value	Cash inflow	DCF factor at 31%	Total present value
1	£3,000	0.800	£2,400	£6,000	0.763	£4,578
2	3,000	0.640	1,920	5,000	0.583	2,915
3	4,000	0.512	2,048	4,000	0.445	1,780
4	9,000	0.410	3,690	2,000	0.340	680
Present value of inflows			10,058			9,953
Initial outlay			10,000			10,000
			£ 58			£ –47
Ranking per IRR			(2)			(1)

Remember: the IRR method requires us to use the rate of interest (DCF factor) which will reduce the net present value of a project to zero.

Figure 12.6 Two mutually exclusive projects: Internal Rate of Return ranking

We can see that the IRR ranking determines our choice to be Project B because it has the higher internal rate of return of 31 per cent compared to Project A, which is 25 per cent.

Thus, use of the NPV method at 10 per cent and the IRR method for ranking projects can provide conflicting results. The reason for this is that the NPV method assumes the cash inflows are reinvested at the rate used to discount, i.e. 10 per cent. By comparison, the IRR method assumes the cash flows are reinvested at the IRR rate, i.e. 25 per cent and 31 per cent respectively for Projects A and B, which may prove to be unrealistic.

The crucial test on which the final acceptance of a project depends is whether or not the IRR compares favourably with the rate of return required by our business. The NPV method is often considered to be the better method since it uses the same discount rate for alternative proposals, and that rate will normally represent the minimum rate acceptable for capital expenditure projects in our business.

The cost of capital

Using discounted cash flow to assess capital projects requires the calculation of our cost of capital. Let us consider why this is so.

A business may obtain funds in a variety of ways, each of which has a different cost associated with it. For instance, it may issue shares and will pay a dividend on those shares, which must represent the cost of raising funds in that way. It may also obtain funds by the issue of debentures (loan certificates as opposed to share certificates or by borrowing from a bank, and in these cases interest is payable. The fact that we may have raised funds in a number of ways makes it more appropriate to use the 'average cost of capital' of our business.

To determine the average cost of capital we need to analyse our capital structure. We can see how to do this in Figure 12.7.

The weighted average cost of capital would in the case of the Tate Restaurant represent the minimum acceptable rate of return for discounted cash flow purposes.

Thus, in summary, because of the large sums of money

involved and the implications associated with the length of time periods, capital expenditure decisions should be carefully evaluated. Discounted cash flow methods provide the appropriate basis for these evaluations because they take into account the time value of money, cash flow and profitability over the entire life of a project.

Source of funds	Proportion of total funds %	Cost of capital %	
Share capital	80	10	800
Loan capital	20	12	240
	100%		1040

The weighted average cost of $= \frac{1040}{100} =$ 10.4 per cent capital

Figure 12.7 The Tate Restaurant. Weighted Average Cost of Capital (WACC) calculation

Present value table

Present value of £1 received at the end of n years ($P = \frac{S}{(1+r)^n}$)

n	1%	2%	3%	4%	5%	6%	7%	8%	9%	10%	11%	12%	13%	14%	15%	n
1	0.990	0.980	0.971	0.962	0.952	0.943	0.935	0.926	0.917	0.909	0.901	0.893	0.885	0.877	0.870	1
2	0.980	0.961	0.943	0.925	0.907	0.890	0.873	0.857	0.842	0.826	0.812	0.797	0.783	0.769	0.756	2
3	0.971	0.942	0.915	0.889	0.864	0.840	0.816	0.794	0.772	0.751	0.731	0.712	0.693	0.675	0.658	3
4	0.961	0.924	0.888	0.855	0.823	0.792	0.763	0.735	0.708	0.683	0.659	0.636	0.613	0.592	0.572	4
5	0.951	0.906	0.863	0.822	0.784	0.747	0.713	0.681	0.650	0.621	0.593	0.567	0.543	0.519	0.497	5
6	0.942	0.888	0.837	0.790	0.746	0.705	0.666	0.630	0.596	0.564	0.535	0.507	0.480	0.456	0.432	6
7	0.933	0.871	0.813	0.760	0.711	0.665	0.623	0.583	0.547	0.513	0.482	0.452	0.425	0.400	0.376	7
8	0.923	0.853	0.789	0.731	0.677	0.627	0.582	0.540	0.502	0.467	0.434	0.404	0.376	0.351	0.327	8
9	0.914	0.837	0.766	0.703	0.645	0.592	0.544	0.500	0.460	0.424	0.391	0.361	0.333	0.308	0.284	9
10	0.905	0.820	0.744	0.676	0.614	0.558	0.508	0.463	0.422	0.386	0.352	0.322	0.295	0.270	0.247	10
11	0.896	0.804	0.722	0.650	0.585	0.527	0.475	0.429	0.388	0.350	0.317	0.287	0.261	0.237	0.215	11
12	0.887	0.788	0.701	0.625	0.557	0.497	0.444	0.397	0.356	0.319	0.286	0.257	0.231	0.208	0.187	12
13	0.879	0.773	0.681	0.601	0.530	0.469	0.415	0.368	0.326	0.290	0.258	0.229	0.204	0.182	0.163	13
14	0.870	0.758	0.661	0.577	0.505	0.442	0.388	0.340	0.299	0.263	0.232	0.205	0.181	0.160	0.141	14
15	0.861	0.743	0.642	0.555	0.481	0.417	0.362	0.315	0.275	0.239	0.209	0.183	0.160	0.140	0.123	15

n	16%	17%	18%	19%	20%	21%	22%	23%	24%	25%	26%	27%	28%	29%	30%	
1	0.862	0.855	0.847	0.840	0.833	0.826	0.820	0.813	0.806	0.800	0.794	0.787	0.781	0.775	0.769	1
2	0.743	0.731	0.718	0.706	0.694	0.683	0.672	0.661	0.650	0.640	0.630	0.620	0.610	0.601	0.592	2
3	0.641	0.624	0.609	0.593	0.579	0.564	0.551	0.537	0.524	0.512	0.500	0.488	0.477	0.466	0.455	3
4	0.552	0.534	0.516	0.499	0.482	0.467	0.451	0.437	0.423	0.410	0.397	0.384	0.373	0.361	0.350	4
5	0.476	0.456	0.437	0.419	0.402	0.386	0.370	0.355	0.341	0.328	0.315	0.303	0.291	0.280	0.269	5
6	0.410	0.390	0.370	0.352	0.335	0.319	0.303	0.289	0.275	0.262	0.250	0.238	0.227	0.217	0.207	6
7	0.354	0.333	0.314	0.296	0.279	0.263	0.249	0.235	0.222	0.210	0.198	0.188	0.178	0.168	0.159	7
8	0.305	0.285	0.266	0.249	0.233	0.218	0.204	0.191	0.179	0.168	0.157	0.148	0.139	0.130	0.123	8
9	0.263	0.243	0.225	0.209	0.194	0.180	0.167	0.155	0.144	0.134	0.125	0.116	0.108	0.101	0.094	9
10	0.227	0.208	0.191	0.176	0.162	0.149	0.137	0.126	0.116	0.107	0.099	0.092	0.085	0.078	0.073	10
11	0.195	0.178	0.162	0.148	0.135	0.123	0.112	0.103	0.094	0.086	0.079	0.072	0.066	0.061	0.056	11
12	0.168	0.152	0.137	0.124	0.112	0.102	0.092	0.083	0.076	0.069	0.062	0.057	0.052			12
13	0.145	0.130	0.116	0.104	0.093	0.084	0.075	0.068	0.061	0.055						13
14	0.125	0.111	0.099	0.088	0.078	0.069	0.062	0.055								14
15	0.108	0.095	0.084	0.074	0.065	0.057	0.051									15

Index